DRAWING PRODUCT IDEAS

FAST AND EASY UX DRAWING FOR ANYONE

KENT EISENHUTH

For general information on our other products and services or for technical support, please contact our Customer Care Department within the United States at (800) 762-2974, outside the United States at (317) 572-3993 or fax (317) 572-4002.

If you believe you've found a mistake in this book, please bring it to our attention by emailing our reader support team at wileysupport@wiley.com with the subject line "Possible Book Errata Submission."

Wiley also publishes its books in a variety of electronic formats. Some content that appears in print may not be available in electronic formats. For more information about Wiley products, visit our web site at www.wiley.com.

Library of Congress Control Number: 2022942897

Cover image: Courtesy of Kent Eisenhuth
Cover design: Wiley

SKY10036054_092022

Past

To my parents, Ned and Nanette, who always encouraged me to develop my drawing skills as a child and well into my adulthood.

Present

To my wife, Beverly, who gave me the courage to write this book and believed in it from its beginning, when it was a nascent idea.

Future

To my kids, Harper and Hudson, whose uninhibited drawings, creativity, and imagination should be an inspiration to us all.

ABOUT THE AUTHOR

 **Kent Eisenhuth** is a Fellow of the Royal Society of Arts. Kent has developed visual languages that improve collaboration, comprehension, and decision-making across a wide array of Google products including Fitbit, Google Cloud, and Alphabet's Loon. Kent leads Google's Data Accessibility program. He previously led Google Cloud's Data Visualization Program and coauthored the data visualization specs for Material Design. Kent's work and ideas have appeared in many publications, including *The Guardian*, *UXmatters*, ACM journals, and *Smashing Magazine*. Kent has presented talks and ideas at many conferences, such as IxDA's Interaction, SXSW, and the Israeli Visualization Conference, and he is a frequent guest lecturer at several universities in the United States.

ACKNOWLEDGMENTS

Writing this book was an extremely difficult yet rewarding experience. I'm forever thankful for all the people who helped me develop this book.

To Beverly Eisenhuth, my wife, who believed in me and offered her unconditional support throughout the process. I couldn't have done this without you.

To Manuel Lima, who encouraged me to write a book on drawing. Manuel's experience and support was insanely helpful throughout the process, and I'm fortunate to have such an amazing mentor.

To Gary Hitzemann, my lifelong mentor who acted as a sounding board during the book's pitch process.

To Darryl Rentz, for his contributions to the pitch and for helping me find the right tone and voice for the book.

To all of my other mentors and colleagues. including Kevin Richardson, Matthew Bartholomew, Rebecca Danna, Hilal Koyuncu, Harold Hambrose, and David Bartel, all of whom helped me develop the book's narrative and suggested areas of focus.

To Clare Cotugno for her help in editing the initial manuscript. More importantly, Clare helped me find my voice as a writer and encouraged me to publish my work early on in my career. She helped me discover my own writing skills. Clare, if it wasn't for you, this book wouldn't exist.

To all the people who helped me develop my drawing skills over the years, including Fredrick Wetzel, Gary Hitzemann, James A Rose, Kevin McCloskey, Marilyn Lehman, Timothy Barr, and Bill Whalen.

To the other authors, artists, architects, and creatives who offered their perspective and peer reviews, including Dr. Neil Cohn, Jason Borbay, Joseph Biondo, Dan Boyarski, David Bullock, Steve Hassard, and Carolyn Knight. Having the opportunity to spend time with you was the most enjoyable part of the whole writing process.

To the amazing publishing team at Wiley, including Jim Minatel, Pete Gaughan, Tracy Brown, and Melissa Burlock. It was an absolute joy working with this team, and I'm forever grateful for their advice, feedback, and help in giving life to this book.

CONTENTS

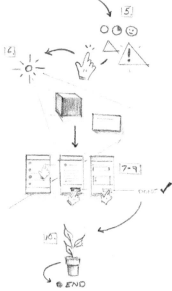

FOREWORD

BY MANUEL LIMA

The ability to draw is embedded in all of us from a very early age. Before we can articulate a single sentence, we are compelled to sketch— random lines and scribbles at first, patterns and geometric shapes as we get older. This early exploration is a foundational step in developing a language of thought while also improving important motor skills. Even if most of us get progressively better during childhood, as we get older, we tend to lose our innate connection to drawing. We consider it too childish or lacking intrinsic value. Or worse, we become self-conscious and start believing we are not good at it. And in the process, we forget how deeply gratifying it can be.

While we spend years in school mastering all possible rules and combinations on how to apply the 26 symbols that make up the alphabet, somehow we assume drawing skills and visual literacy should come naturally to us, without any specific training or focused practice. It is therefore not surprising that most of us eventually distance ourselves from our innate ability to draw with our hands. Such detachment appears more acute within the tech industry, where every so often a new digital tool comes around to fulfill our desire for visual depiction in unpredictable ways. Packed with extravagant pen styles, fanciful shapes, outlines, and transitions, modern-day digital tools make hand drawing seem like a thing of the past.

Repeatedly, I see designers jumping straight to the latest digital tool, enamored by its shiny new features, without thinking deeply about what they are creating in the first place and considering the various interdependent parts that make up their grand idea. This can lead to a lot of wasted time. Using pen and paper is not just important to think through scenarios before committing to a solution, it is often the most liberating step in your iteration process. If you don't allow yourself this key step, your idea becomes immediately conditioned by the tool's capabilities. I'm often asked what tool I recommend for design and data visualization. The answer is always obvious: pen and paper.

Kent's book is a fabulous guide in this context. It teaches us how to bring the pen and paper back into the lives of user experience designers and digital product creators. Whether you are developing a new user interface for a website, mobile application, service, TV system, or game console, this book will be instrumental for you to structure and articulate your ideas while building your own combinatorial visual language. In the process, not only will you save countless hours redoing wireframes and final interface mocks, but you will also discover the true power of an unconstrained creative mind.

PREFACE

I spent most of my childhood drawing and painting. As I was growing up, I aspired to be an architect. I was obsessed with buildings. Figure 1 depicts a random architectural doodle I created back then. After completing an independent study with a local architect and mentor, I quickly learned how to refine my drawing skills and create a visual style that enabled me to pitch new and exciting ideas.

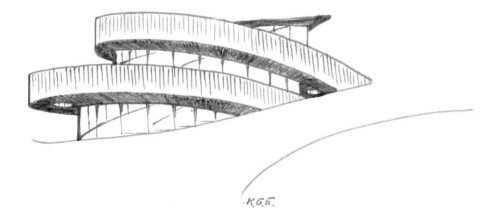

FIGURE 1

For various reasons, I never achieved my goal of becoming an architect. However, I found my way into User Experience (UX) design. Throughout my career, I've carried a lot of the ideas, principles, and techniques I learned from childhood, and I've spent a lot of time refining them. My drawing style is a combination of techniques I applied in watercolor painting, drafting, and digital design. The drawing in Figure 2 is a fine example of how I combined these various techniques. As a result of blending these skills and techniques, I've experienced a lot of success sharing ideas early and often.

Drawing has improved the quality of ideas explored by the teams on which I've worked. I've been able to successfully apply drawing in a way that enabled me to challenge the status quo, explore new ideas, and share the breadth of my thinking. I've used drawing to enable my teams to align on ideas that we co-created.

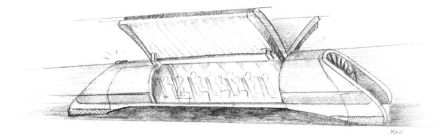

FIGURE 2

For example, I used hand-drawn sketches to design one of the first mobile and web apps for controlling lights and shades in homes. I also used drawing and sketching to convince a customer to drastically change the way in which scientists interact with an atomic force microscope. One of my early atomic force microscope concept drawings is displayed in Figure 3.

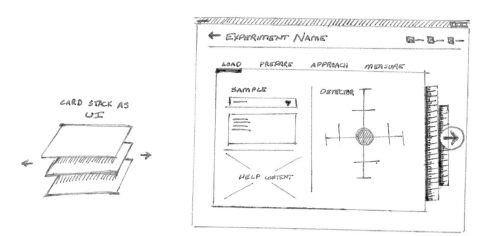

FIGURE 3

Later in my career, I used hand-drawn sketches to help pitch Rivet, an AI-powered reading skills practice app offered by Google. I also used drawings to enable the team, a group of non-designers, to explore some early minimum viable product, or MVP, designs for the app.

Finally, I successfully created a hand-drawn presentation to convince a Google Cloud team to shift from a text-driven interface to a visual interface that used visualizations to highlight insights within the data.

I want to share my success with you, and I truly believe that my style and technique doesn't require artistic talent to master. I'm confident that with a few quick and easy adjustments to your drawing technique, you will be able to draw digital product designs, like the one in Figure 4, with finesse, polish, and confidence. Most importantly, you can start creating more impactful designs with your team.

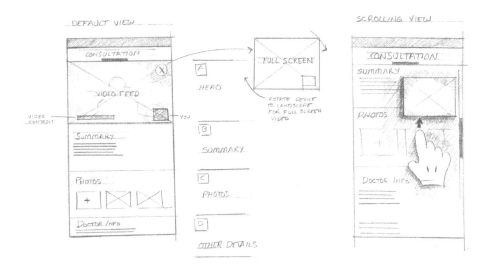

FIGURE 4

INTRODUCTION

Do you find drawing unapproachable or intimidating? A lot of people do, and for good reason. Drawing gets a bad rap. Most people think you have to be an artist or seasoned designer to be able to do it well. They believe that it requires formal training. This is definitely not true.

If you create digital products and you're not a designer, you have a reason to read this book. By sharing everything I've learned throughout the years, I'm hoping to empower you to channel your artistic skills and include drawing and sketching in your everyday process. It's a fact that the human brain processes images more quickly than it processes words. Images are the essential language we use when sharing and collaborating on new ideas. As people who design and build digital products, we will continue to rely on this as the design problems we tackle become more complex and as design thinking continues to gain popularity.

Do you work on digital products? Do you consider yourself a designer? If not, do you want to contribute to the creative process? It turns out that you can and should. In fact, you can be good at it, too. As design problems become more complex, designers are relying on teammates like you to help co-design solutions. I truly believe that everyone is a designer and the best ideas are built in a group. The success of your team's product might depend on your input, and drawing can be your ticket to success.

Are you already a seasoned designer? Is drawing a key part of your process? If so, this book will enable you to build confidence in your drawing ability. It will provide methods for getting your colleagues on board with your process so you can all become better collaborators.

If you're not a designer, you have even better reasons to read this book.

Are you a subject matter expert? If so, you can use drawing to ensure your team's designers are seeing and understanding your domain-specific point of view. For them, it's important that your expertise shines through in the end product.

Are you a researcher? If so, you can use drawing to ensure your user experience (UX) research and requirements are well represented in your team's final product. If you work in a siloed organization, drawing will help you blur the lines between you and your design counterparts.

Are you going to build the product? Are you an engineer or developer? If so, you may use drawing to co-design an end solution that is useful, exciting, and fits within identified technical requirements and constraints.If you can draw boxes and arrows similar to the ones displayed here, you have what it takes to draw a design—and a good one for that matter. Remember, in order to draw with your team, you don't have to be a critically acclaimed artist, nor do you have to be a designer.

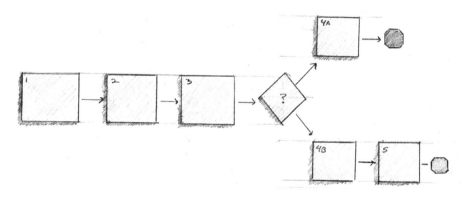

FIGURE 5

So what do you think? Are you ready to get started? If so, let's jump in.

CHAPTER ONE

WHY DRAW?

Great digital products start with great design. A great design isn't created in a vacuum. It takes time, research, and the unique perspective of many contributors along the way. I've always viewed the design process as a form of problem solving, and as technology advances, the problems become more complex. As a result, our teammates from all functional areas are participating in this process, whether they realize it or not.

Throughout this process, drawing is the key method for developing, testing, and collaborating on new ideas, and there are several benefits to including drawing in your product development process, as illustrated in the mind map in Figure 1.1.

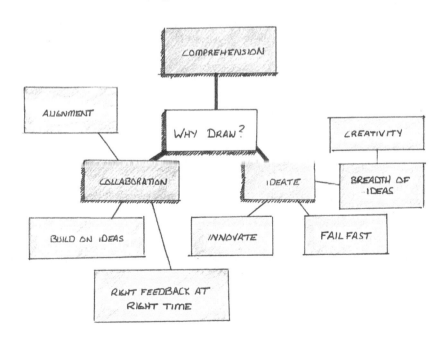

FIGURE 1.1

Drawings attract people to an idea. It's true that a picture is worth a thousand words, and drawing has withstood the test of time, having been used as an effective communications tool for tens of thousands of years. This isn't an exaggeration. Figure 1.2 is a recreation of a drawing from the rock shelters of Bhimbetka. Some of the drawings in these shelters are considered to be 30,000 years old. In today's digital age, drawing is not only still relevant but needed more than ever.

FIGURE 1.2
Source: Based on Bhimbetka drawings (Kent Eisenhuth)

Drawing is a quick and easy way to start putting form to an early idea. Let's go back to our original mind map of the benefits of drawing and further examine the three main types of benefits that come from including drawing in your product development process.

EXPLORE AN IDEA

Drawing is a low-risk exercise that allows you to rapidly work through many concepts. Early in the process, I usually start with some quick doodles. The focus on quantity over quality helps me clear out initial biases, and it forces me to think of alternate solutions. It brings me closer to the problem at hand, because thinking about alternative ideas causes the creative juices to flow.

Usually my first few ideas are bad before they're even penned. It's usually my fourth, fifth, and sixth doodles that represent ideas that begin to hold water.

I'm not alone in this line of thinking. As my former professor David Bullock used to say, there's nothing quite like developing an idea through mind, hand, and paper. Putting a multitude of ideas down on paper instead of focusing on the first thing that comes to mind leads to a better solution. Breadth in thinking enables you to discover connections between two seemingly disconnected ideas, which can lead you to focusing on the right answer.

In doing this, I found that it's important to get the bad ideas down on paper first so I can open up the headspace to focus on other, more thoughtful ideas. Most of my doodles have a long-standing date with the trash can, and they never see the light of day. They're merely chicken scratch and that's okay. I'm the only one who has to understand them at this point in the process. Once seeing the idea on paper, I can better understand why it might not work, learn from it, and move on to a better idea. I learn a lot from these quick doodles. In Figure 1.3 you can see some quick doodles I created to help me explore some ideas for visualizing an organizational structure within a company.

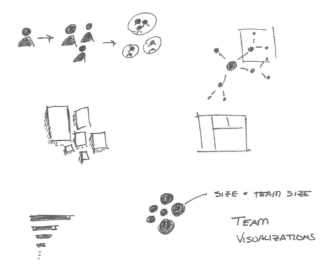

FIGURE 1.3

At one point, I was working on a website that would shed light on the digital divide in America. Our goal was to highlight segments in the American population that live in urban and rural areas alike. We wanted to spotlight critical issues affecting these areas that were caused by a lack of high-speed Internet access.

The first goal was to compare the two categories. To do this, the first and most obvious way was to show two tables side by side as drawn in

Figure 1.4. One table would list all the urban counties, their populations, and the number of people without Internet access. The second would focus on the rural counties and do the same. During this process, I knew I wanted to get the obvious ideas down on paper first.

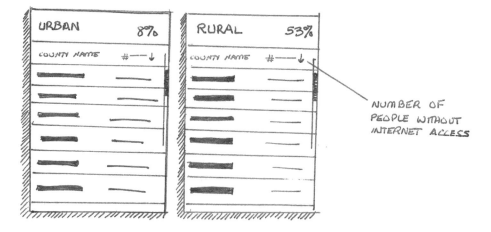

FIGURE 1.4

Once I was able to get the obvious down on paper, I was able to think more clearly about the information we wanted to share and how it would support the underlying story. As a result, I started to think about how different charts and graphs might be used to display the information in a more insightful way.

For example, I explored how a graph might help us compare access rates across the two categories. Additionally, I wanted to explore where the most affected people are located. Finally, I wanted to see how resulting issues affected the populations in each category. My later explorations, as depicted in Figure 1.5, represent concepts that uncover more of these insights. I was even able to explore a few experimental ideas just so that I could start the right conversations with my teammates and project stakeholders.

Drawing enables you to quickly explore alternate, possibly better ways to solve the problem at hand. It can help you understand when and why you should break the rules of your company's underlying design guidelines and not just use an out-of-the-box component available to you.

Drawing can help you intimately connect with the problem you're trying to solve and explore a range of solutions that provide a range of benefits to your product's users. Too many times this part of the process is overlooked, and it shows in the end result. Product teams should never be happy with the status quo. We need to push the boundaries of our work. Let me ask you this, Do you want to create a product that meets expectations or exceeds them?

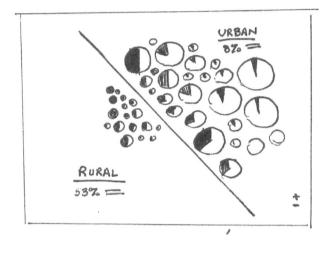

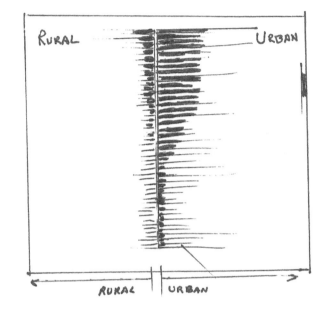

FIGURE 1.5

GAIN A SHARED UNDERSTANDING

Drawing is essential to comprehension. A picture will resonate with your audience more than a long explanation. Remember, the earliest forms of communication were drawings. Early written languages often used pictograms to capture history, ideas, and concepts. With the growing use of emojis and pictures in our text communications, it almost feels like we're getting back to that.

Recently I had a chance to catch up with Professor Dan Boyarski, a professor emeritus at Carnegie Mellon University. During our chat, he was describing a guest lecture he gave to a class at CMU's business school. Before he started his lecture, he tried to engage the business students by asking them to discuss a project they were working on. For this project, both individuals and teams were working on solving complex business problems. Professor Boyarski asked if anyone wanted to describe their problem.

An individual stood up by his seat and spent about two to three minutes explaining his project. At the end of it, Professor Boyarski asked the class if they all understood the problem and if it was clear. He explained that most of the students were quiet and didn't really respond.

Another volunteer stood up and asked if he could use his chair as a visual aid. He moved to the center aisle in the lecture hall and explained the problem his team was trying to solve. He went on to explain that a lot of people drive to work. Once they're at the office, their car sits for hours in a lot. His team was wondering how people without cars could use the idle cars to drive to meetings and other events out of the office. Each time he referred to the parked car, he pointed to the chair. At the end of his explanation, Professor Boyarski asked the business students if they understood the problem. This time several students nodded, and when asked why, the students answered, "Because he used his chair."

As the story goes, Professor Boyarski asked a third group to explain the problem they were solving, but this time use the available whiteboards in the room to explain it. A volunteer from this group described her group's project. She explained how they were looking at the barges going up and down the three rivers surrounding Pittsburgh. As she began to speak, she drew lines representing the three rivers as depicted in Figure 1.6.

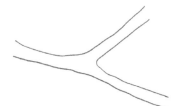

FIGURE 1.6

Then she described how there are locks located on each river. As she was talking, she drew locks across each of the three rivers. She described how barges traveling in each direction have to travel through these locks. She drew boxes representing the barges at each lock station as highlighted in Figure 1.7.

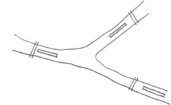

FIGURE 1.7

She went on to describe how each lock includes a little building, so she drew huts to represent the buildings. In each building there are a few people that manage traffic through the lock. This is necessary since you can only let one barge pass through the lock at a time. She drew people next to each of the huts as depicted in Figure 1.8.

FIGURE 1.8

She said, "Our project is to look at an efficient and cost-effective way for these people to talk to each other as they control barge traffic on the rivers." She drew lines connecting all the people across the different locks, shown in Figure 1.9.

Once she put down her marker, the audience applauded. When Professor Boyarski asked the business students why they applauded, they described how the student told a story through building a drawing in a way that they could all quickly understand the problem at hand. Instead of talking about the problem, she showed it.

This student used drawing to help her colleagues understand the problem and opened up the door for ideas and collaboration.

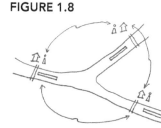

FIGURE 1.9

IMPROVE COLLABORATION

In addition to using it as a tool to aid comprehension, we use drawing to build on each other's ideas. As design thinking becomes a mainstream practice, we find ourselves making key product decisions at the whiteboard. At some companies, design thinking is the centerpiece of the product development process. At Google, we use design sprints to create solutions for complex design problems. Our cross-functional teammates spend a lot of time drawing and ideating with us designers. Key product decisions are made during these sessions, and drawing is the main collaboration tool used to ideate and build consensus across our teams. It's a low-risk activity that drives alignment on an idea before a lot of time, resources, and work are invested in it. I'll share more on this later on.

ANYONE CAN DRAW

Drawing is a means to an end. Your goal is not to create the best drawing, it's to contribute to the best possible outcome for your team's product. But even with this in mind, why is drawing so intimidating?

According to Joseph Biondo, FAIA, professor of architecture at Lafayette University and author of *House Equanimity*, we stop drawing at an early age. As Professor Biondo explains, when we were children, our peers, parents, and teachers started providing feedback on our early and primitive drawings. Because of this, we limited our skills and crushed our creative spirit, and in most cases, we gave up. This is why the majority of us have the drawing skills of a young child. As far as this book is concerned, our drawings only have to be good enough to hang up on our kitchen refrigerator, or "refrigerator museum" as he puts it.

JOSEPH BIONDO, FAIA, ON THE VALUE OF DRAWING

Early in my career, I had the privilege of working with Joseph Biondo, professor of architecture at Lafayette College, author of *House Equanimity* (Oscar Riera Ojeda Publisher, 2018) and AIA Fellow. Here's what he had to say on the value of drawing, overcoming the fear of jumping into it, and its role as a communications tool in the process.

He encourages everyone to draw immediately and stresses the need to go back to the renaissance time, when things were built with higher purpose. People used hands and minimal drawings to convey what needed to be done. "Everyone was an artist." Since then, the process of making has become much too complex. He advocates keeping it primal and simple. He explained the minimalism in construction drawings. People would just draw on the wall of the house to work through the problem with the contractor. When these people drew, it ensured the process was totally integrated and everyone was working together.

Drawings are especially valuable in the early stages of design. Drawing with a pencil enables greater control of the line. The illustration above provides a good example of this claim. The texture of the paper is important because it affects the line. The ambiguity created by lines on the paper is important and leaves room for more conversation and dialog with peers. If you show a high-fidelity, finite drawing, you're missing out on an opportunity for this type of discussion. He refers to this overly worked drawing as choreographed collaboration.

According to Joe, most students are intimidated when staring at the blank canvas, sketchbook, or whiteboard. He asks them to draw a deliberate line. This is a metaphor to the mark you leave in life. Are you going to be timid about it? You have to approach it with curiosity and zeal. It's important to practice drawing and do it often.

By not focusing on creating the perfect drawing, you'll free up the headspace to focus more on the idea you're trying to communicate, and you'll automatically become better at drawing. Would you like to see this in practice? Let's try something out. Grab a sheet of paper and a pen.

Draw a few quick scribbles. You don't have to think about it. Just do it. Figure 1.10 provides a few example squiggles to get you started.

Next, can you draw a wedge and a dot as depicted in Figure 1.11? Try it out.

Add a dot and a wedge shape to each of your scribbles and voilà! You just drew a flock of birds! Figure 1.12 provides a few examples.

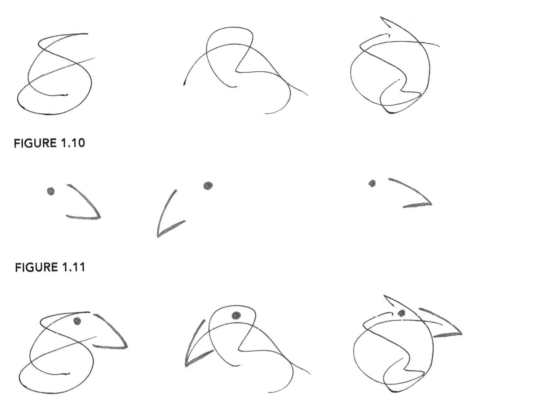

FIGURE 1.10

FIGURE 1.11

FIGURE 1.12

Not sure how to turn your scribble into a bird drawing? You might have to be creative in how you add your wedges. Check out Figure 1.13 for some inspiration. Sometimes a picture frame helps too!

FIGURE 1.13

So what do you think? Did it work for you? This exercise is called Squiggle Birds, and it is an example of a warm-up exercise I've used during cross-functional design workshops to get everyone in the right mood to start drawing and exploring new product ideas. Not only is this a great warm-up exercise, it's a good method for proving that anyone can draw. Thank you to my friend, mentor, and fellow Googler Vaishali Jain, who introduced me to this activity years ago.

If you're on a plane heading across the United States to your next meeting, you should be able to vastly improve your drawing skills before you land. You can even start practicing the ideas and concepts described in this book and draw along with me. By doing this, you'll supercharge the collaboration skills you'll be using in your upcoming meeting.

RIGHT TIME AND PLACE

Before we go any further, let's take a minute to acknowledge something. Drawing has its time and place. Doodling and drawing are fine tools to employ at any point in your design process. That said, there are times where it works better than others. Here are a few instances when drawing can lead to a great outcome.

In the Beginning

I rely on drawing very early in the design process. It works really well when we're just starting to give form to solutions to a large, ambiguous problem. I'll draw a mind map or a diagram that helps me organize my thoughts and understand the problem space. I'll draw a process diagram to help me understand the journey of a user and to better empathize with them.

Once I have a few ideas in mind, I'll use drawing to explore a range of ways in which a product can solve the problem at hand. Usually this is a visualization concept or a flow of screen proposals. I'll explore conservative and edgier ideas alike. It's typical for a designers to develop 30 or more drawings per day during this phase of the process (Buxton 2007, 160). At this point in the process, it's all about exploring as many ideas as possible. It's a low-risk activity after all.

Once I have some of these big ideas down on paper, I usually include another designer and researcher in my process. I like to sketch with them so we can build on each other's ideas. It's also a good early sanity check for me. My sketches are typically gestural and leave a lot to the imagination, and that's by design. I'm trying to invite others to build on my ideas. I've found some of my best design work has started in sketching sessions with one or two other colleagues.

During Workshops

As previously mentioned, drawing is an essential collaboration tool. Sometimes collaboration takes place in the form of design sprints and workshops. Carolyn Knight and Steve Hassard are two design sprint leaders at Google. If you're not familiar with design sprints, it's essentially a version of an extended design workshop. Carolyn and Steve have sprinted with countless teams inside and outside of the company. One thing they confirmed is that drawing is essential to the sprint process. In fact, it fits into most stages of the sprint process. You may already know this if you're familiar with the Google Ventures design sprint process and the book *Sprint, How to Solve Big Problems and Test Ideas in Just Five Days* by Jake Knapp, John Zeratsky, and Braden Kowitz (Simon & Schuster, 2016).

According to Carolyn and Steve, drawing is key to many aspects of the design sprint, starting with the day one icebreaker activity. Icebreakers are a good way to break down the barriers to drawing. As the sprint progresses, they are invaluable to get engineers into drawing. For the people who aren't designers in the room, an activity like this pushes them to where they need to be.

As the workshop continues, the drawings help people understand which seemingly disparate ideas can neatly fit together. I've also been involved in countless sprints and workshops. During these activities, it's really interesting to see the cross-pollination of ideas and the consensus forming around one or two big ideas.

According to Carolyn and Steve, some form of drawing is used in nearly every sprint, and seeing these drawings enables people to better understand how the pieces of an idea best fit together. In this case, drawing is a magical tool that enables this to happen. It's amazing to see great ideas unfold in these sessions, and it has been a go-to method for my own design process.

To Facilitate Conversations

Drawing can also enable you to facilitate a conversation on a complex topic as discussed in the earlier story of Professor Boyarski's lecture (Figures 1.6 through 1.9). It's a way of informally showing and not telling. When I worked in consulting, I applied design to many complex business problems.

I remember working with a large logistics and truck rental company. We were helping them rethink the driver experience. During a few informal discussions with key executives, we were sharing our research and findings. The conversation was becoming very complex, and I found the group was getting lost in thought. People's eyes were glazing over and others were just blindly arguing their points.

As a result, I started a mind map of our ideas. Keep in mind, whiteboarding was not part of the culture of this particular client. At the time, I thought I wasn't adding any value to the conversation at hand, and I was just doodling some nonsense on a whiteboard. During the conversation, the executive team started pointing to my sketch and referencing it in their conversation. At one point, the president of the client's logistics division got out of his seat and redrew most of my drawings. At the time, I was mad at myself for not understanding the problem space.

During a quick break in the conversation, my mentor, Matthew Bartholomew, who had witnessed the scene, explained that I shouldn't be mad at myself and that it was a big deal for these people to start drawing on top of my mind map. Apparently this was something he had never witnessed in a meeting before.

When the conversation continued, other executives followed suit. It was amazing to see how the other people started adding to my drawing and using it as a communications tool for facilitating and organizing their thoughts. What I originally thought was nonsense turned out to add a lot of value.

This experience helped me realize that drawing is such a versatile tool. I also realized that I needed to brush up on my showmanship at the whiteboard, because I planned on doing this more often—especially for those that don't consider themselves "whiteboarding types."

Unbuttoning the Process

Digital designers and producers, really anyone working in User Experience (UX), love a good process. Sometimes these processes become too buttoned up. It's important to have fun, and drawing is a way to do so. Sometimes a few quirky doodles give your work the personality it needs. Who knows? Maybe that squiggly bird you drew earlier will find its way into your next design presentation.

Having fun with drawing is a great way to unbutton the process and enable your colleagues, partners, and stakeholders to loosen up and join in on the creative process. When we're all having fun, we do our best work.

Eliciting the Right Kind of Feedback

If the process is done right, you'll receive a lot of constructive feedback from your team. The low fidelity of a drawing implies that your idea isn't fully baked and that you're looking for feedback. When designers show high-fidelity computer-generated mockups, the rest of the team is more likely to focus on the finer details, and they don't provide feedback on the foundational idea you're trying to build upon.

A few years ago, I was working on redesigning a very prominent cloud product. We were rebuilding the experience from the ground up. Early on, we used drawing to explore many new ideas, capture the product's information architecture, and explore some new patterns for navigating the product. As I was presenting the drawings to the stakeholder team, a very prominent engineering director interrupted me just to thank me for showing drawings and nothing more. After this, I noticed members of his team perking up and actively providing feedback and building on our ideas. It was a great moment, although I was surprised that the team hadn't been sharing preliminary drawings or process work in the past.

CAROLYN KNIGHT & STEVE HASSARD: GOOGLE SPRINT LEADERS

During my time with them, the Google sprint leaders shared several anecdotes and stories. It became clear that drawing is an essential part of sprint culture. Here's more on what they had to say during our conversation.

Tell us about the role of drawing in the design sprint process.

It starts with the icebreaker. In one case, sprint participants were asked to draw a portrait of the person next to them. Initially, this request really freaked people out. There was that moment where everyone was looking at each other like "can we not do this?" Once people pushed through the exercise, then saw the other person's reaction to it, the energy fundamentally changed in the room. For a cross-functional group, this activity pushed them to where they needed to be and opened the door for enriched collaboration later in the sprint.

When people are comfortable drawing, it's a sign that people can be more open and creative. It's good to get people out of their element and push them a little. If they're not doing drawings, the design turns into a requirements list or bill of materials, which don't help anyone. The pictures are worth a thousand words, which is better for moving quickly, especially when people from different functional areas such as engineering and product management are working alongside the design team.

Tell us about a time when drawing helped a diverse group gain a shared understanding of a difficult problem.

During the Hacking Health conference, we organized a sprint to design an app for case workers. We brought in other general stakeholders. Some worked in education, some were caseworkers, and so on. Drawing facilitated a shared understanding of the problem space across an array of people and backgrounds including doctors, nurses, caseworkers, people working in education, and general stakeholders. The team drew a map of the problem space. The visual of this map was important because without it, the conversation was all over the place.

Tell us about a time when drawing enabled people to collectively add to a new idea.

We ran a sprint with the City of San Jose to improve the 311 and 911 call center experience. In this case, it took some time for the participants to get into the groove of ideating without getting bogged down by potential bureaucratic constraints imposed by the city government.

By drawing, the participants were able to have their own heads-down time, no matter how "impossible" their ideas would be. Once these ideas were shared, it enabled the collective group to start riffing on the ideas and get into the right brainstorming mode. This wouldn't have happened if it wasn't for the individual drawing time because people would have had an opportunity to interrupt and shoot down an idea prematurely.

Challenging the Status Quo

For this last point, I'm going to get on my soapbox for a minute. If you're a designer, please make note of this. Drawing unlocks a part of the process that has been getting lost in recent years. Yes, this is true, and please hear me out on this one.

More often than not, the design of most digital products is based on some sort of component library. It's very tempting to jump right into using your library's predefined patterns, components, and sticker sheets. It's easy for designers to fall into the rut of jumping into creating high-fidelity designs by using canned templates, patterns, and designs already provided. Some designers thrive on this, and they insist this is the way to go. While that might work for very minor additions to mature products, it doesn't work when starting a new challenge. In my opinion, opportunities are missed when this happens.

CHAPTER TWO

REFRAMING OUR THINKING

Historically, drawing has been perceived as an inherited talent. We grew up under the impression that in order to draw, we must be able to create an accurate representation of the objects in the environment around us. Being able to take a blank canvas or sheet of paper and draw an accurate representation of a complex image takes a tremendous amount of talent, and those who have figured out how to do it well are true artists. That said, this perception of drawing has hindered our ability as adults to try it for ourselves.

One of the best ways to get started with drawing is to jump in and start. Let's first create a few drawings. Bear with me through this, because it will take a few minutes to get through. Incidentally, this is an exercise introduced by Manuel Lima, which we like to share with attendees of our data visualization workshops, and it is based on the work of Santiago Ortiz and his article "45 Ways To Represent Two Quantities." Please locate and grab the nearest pen and paper. I want you to think about two numbers in Figure 2.1.

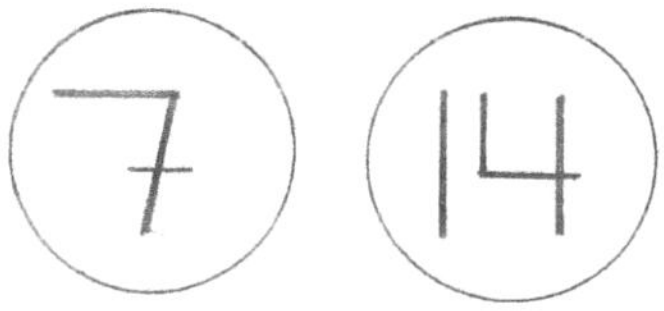

How many ways can you represent these values? Take a few minutes to think about it and jot down a few ideas in your sketchpad. There's no wrong answer to this question. This exercise is meant to inspire divergent thinking. Just as in digital product design and UX, we often explore many concepts and ideas for solving the same problem. We're going to apply that same thinking in this exercise and come up with many ways to visualize these two values.

Try to come up with a new drawing every minute. There's no wrong answer to this. If you think your idea will work, try it. You'll be surprised at what you come up with toward the end of the exercise. Jot down a few ideas, then turn the page.

FIGURE 2.1

15

FIGURE 2.2

FIGURE 2.3

There are endless ways to represent these values. Here are a few of my own explorations. I started by representing 7 and 14 using alternate characters, such as the Roman numerals displayed in Figure 2.2.

Another familiar way to represent these values is to use a series of ticks and slashes. Each slash represents a multiple of 5 as depicted by Figure 2.3. If you enjoy board games as much as I do, you'll recognize that this is a common way to keep score in some games.

In Figure 2.4, I turned the lines into something more abstract, like points. I used basic Gestalt principles to create a visual grouping of the dots. The first cluster has seven points. The second cluster has 14.

So what do you think? Here's another example—instead of using points, I used basic shapes, like the interlocking triangles displayed in Figure 2.5.

FIGURE 2.4

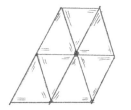

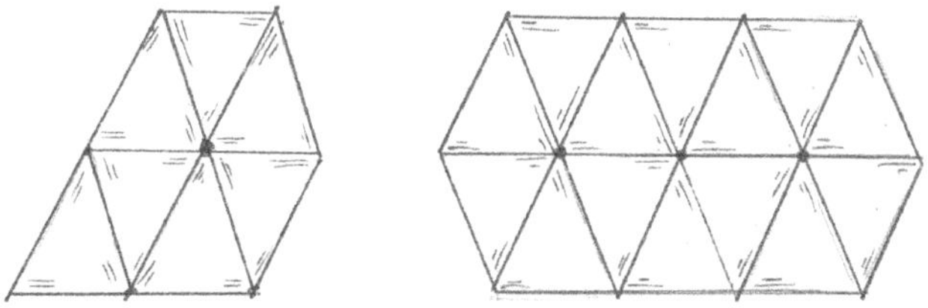

FIGURE 2.5

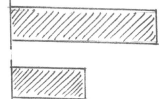

FIGURE 2.6

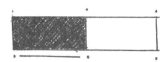

FIGURE 2.7

Now, let's think about the relationship between the two numbers. I considered using basic elements, such as lines of varying lengths. One line might be half the length of the other, since half of 14 is 7, as depicted by Figure 2.6. I even combined them into one shape that is split in half as shown in Figure 2.7.

I thought about representing these values as time. I depicted 700 and 1400 hours by drawing a clock as you see in Figure 2.8. This might seem a bit edgier and abstract, but it still works. What do you think?

Looking at these examples, we can probably agree that they're all unique. That said, these divergent concepts all have more in common than you might think. I'm going to go out on a limb and guess that all of your drawings can be distilled down to the same basic shapes and marks. These basic shapes and marks are part of a primitive visual vocabulary we developed for describing the two values. In this chapter, we will take a closer look and break down each example from the exercise.

FIGURE 2.8

BREAKING IT DOWN

I've distilled all of my representations of 7 and 14 down to the collage of shapes pictured in Figure 2.9. Take a look at the elements within the collage. Can you find them in the exercise examples? Let's take a closer look.

FIGURE 2.9

The Roman numerals were made up of connected lines. The arrows in Figure 2.10 point to the basic shapes and marks in the collage that I used to draw the Roman numeral.

FIGURE 2.10

I drew clusters of points, one consisting of seven points and the other consisting of 14. The arrows in Figure 2.11 highlight the elements used in this representation of the two values. In this case, a point was reused multiple times.

FIGURE 2.11

In one case, I drew a primitive set of shapes. I used a set of 7 and 14 interlocking triangles to represent the two values, as depicted in Figure 2.12.

FIGURE 2.12

When visualizing the relationship between 7 and 14, I drew two boxes, as shown in Figure 2.13. The second is half the length of the first, representing the two values. I added some shading to my boxes to give the drawing some energy and flair; however, that wasn't necessary.

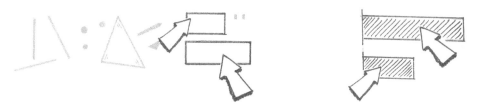

FIGURE 2.13

I think you get the idea. Can you find the shapes used in the clock drawing in Figure 2.14. These basic lines, points, and shapes are part of a basic vocabulary of a primitive visual language I developed to represent the values of 7 and 14.

FIGURE 2.14

I'd like to encourage you to think about how you might combine the shapes in Figure 2.15 in other ways to represent the values of 7 and 14. If you put your mind to it, you'll find that the possibilities are endless.

FIGURE 2.15

INTRODUCING THE SYSTEM

When it comes to drawing digital experiences, **_drawing is a means to an end_**. It serves its purpose in the product development process. You can use it to bring clarity to your own ideas, and you can use it as a tool for development, alignment, collaboration, and sharing. It's a valuable tool that supports the ultimate outcomes we're striving to achieve. It doesn't take talent to draw well enough to accomplish these things within your team, and as demonstrated by the Squiggle Birds exercise in Chapter 1, "Why Draw?," anyone can draw.

During the first 15 years of my professional career, I started to realize that I was reusing the same basic symbols to draw my digital product ideas. You may have realized the same when analyzing your drawings of the quantities 7 and 14. While I thought my drawings were utter trash (I was professionally trained as an artist), I noticed I received a lot of compliments from my design colleagues on how well my drawings were crafted and how well they communicated my ideas.

It became apparent that my system for drawing was effective. Later in my career, I started researching this idea of drawing as a system. As I started researching the topic, I realized several authors and scholars have billed drawing as a visual language. Languages are examples of systems, and I realized my hypotheses and assumptions of my own work were leading me somewhere.

As I continued looking into this, I came across the research and writings of Dr. Neil Cohn, founder of Visual Language Lab and author of *The Visual Language of Comics* (Bloomsbury Academic, 2014). Dr. Cohn validated a lot of my own thoughts in how I approached drawing in my day-to-day work. He proposes that drawings are made up of visual vocabulary that possess a regularized and/or iconic meaning among a group of people. In our case, we're working with people who design and build digital products.

DR. NEIL COHN: DRAWING AS A VISUAL LANGUAGE

D r. Cohn explains drawing as a visual language. Incidentally, a language is a great example of a system. Languages are made up of several words that can be combined and structured to convey meaning. There are endless ways to combine words. Over the years, several scholars have viewed drawing as a visual language. Drawings are made up of a series of basic shapes that possess a regularized and/or iconic meaning among a group of people. Additionally, you can apply structure and a basic visual grammar to the images for conveying information and storytelling.

Dr. Cohn teaches a drawing course at Tilburg University in the Netherlands. Over the years, he has fine-tuned the way in which he introduces drawing to his students. First he'll ask the students this: "Can you speak?" The response from the class is an overwhelming *yes*. Next, he'll ask what they speak in. This question is met with a range of answers, usually types of languages, including English, Spanish, German, and so on. So the next question becomes this: "Can you draw? What do you draw in?" The answers to these two questions are usually all over the place. First of all, not everyone believes they can draw. According to Dr. Cohn, we don't have a parallel set of answers to these two sets of questions and the answers to these questions are asymmetrical.

When speaking a particular language like French, English, or Spanish, we pull words from our vocabulary that enable us to speak. If we think of drawing as a language, then there's an underlying vocabulary that comes with it. The languages also have a particular structure and grammar that come with them.

So how might this apply to digital products? For those of us working in this space, we speak in "digital products." Our visual vocabulary is made up of symbols and shapes that we're already familiar with, such as UI components, screens, and people—graphical units that we're already working with on a regular basis. If we can become comfortable with drawing these basic units, we are on our way to building our own visual vocabulary within the digital product visual language.

Assuming our visual language is UX or digital product design, our drawings will be made up of shapes that resemble the elements we interact with in most apps. As depicted by Figure 2.16, some of these elements might be screen-based, including form fields, buttons, check boxes, mouse cursors, lists, tables, and charts.

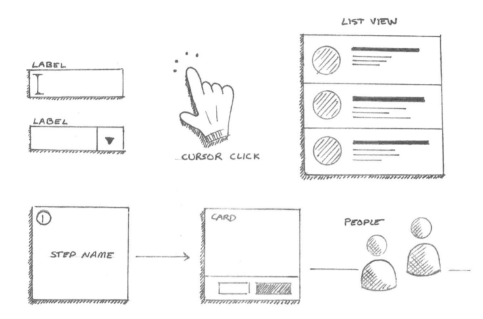

FIGURE 2.16

In other cases, as also depicted in Figure 2.17, we'll need to draw non-screen-based elements to tell a story about our idea. This might include basic people figures, devices, and an assortment of diagrams that will enable us to organize our thoughts and research. This is the start of our drawing system. Now, let's compare drawing to another system, one that I think is more fun.

FIGURE 2.17

I like to compare drawing to a popular construction toy. Legos were a huge part of my childhood. In fact, I had 56 Lego sets fully constructed in my parents' basement. The space was a maker's dream. In fact, in the 1980s, did you know that Lego actually called itself Lego System? That is because they are indeed a system. Did you know that you can combine 6 standard 4x2 Lego bricks (Figure 2.18) in over 915 million combinations (Eilers, 2005)?

FIGURE 2.18

Lego offers several standard brick types in varying configurations. Each brick has its own purpose. There are 1x1, 2x1, 2x2, 3x2, and 4x2 configurations. Brick shapes may include cylinders, squares, rectangles, and triangles. These pieces can be combined in infinite ways to build any sort of model we can dream up. When we see the end result, we experience the model as a whole—the sum of the parts, as shown in Figure 2.19.

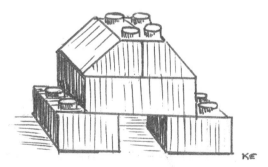

FIGURE 2.19

A great product drawing should enable us to focus on the solution as a whole—the sum of the parts. Now, let's think about the very primitive icons, shapes, and symbols that we might use to represent the basic UI elements found in our digital products. If we think about these elements as our Lego bricks, as suggested in Figure 2.20, we can combine them in infinite ways to share and collaborate on any digital product idea, just as we can combine Lego bricks in infinite ways to make any model we wish.

FIGURE 2.20

I think we can all get behind these metaphors and consider drawing a system. If I asked you to think about how to break a product drawing into some basic, reusable, Lego brick-like parts, you might have difficulty in doing so. You might have the same feeling people get when sitting in front of a blank canvas attempting to draw a real-world object. Once you know what to look for, it becomes easy.

COMMON DRAWINGS

I'm going to share a few common UX drawings in a style that has worked for me, and I'll break them down into their metaphorical Lego bricks. If you create and build digital experiences, then you'll likely use these drawings in your day-to-day work with your product team. Here are a few types of drawings nearly every digital product design process includes. In fact, if you work in the field, you've probably already seen them. Let's take a look at what they're used for and then how they can be deconstructed.

Site Maps

Site maps are similar to mind maps. Their top-down hierarchical layout helps us understand proposed navigation schemes and the organization of content. In Figure 2.21 we see a mapping of the screens that make up a mobile health tracking app.

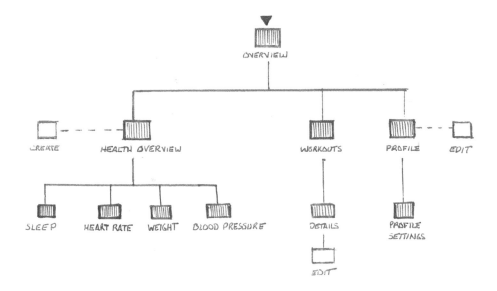

FIGURE 2.21

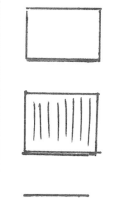

This diagram is made up of boxes and lines. In this case, I used a texture made up of vertical lines to highlight screens with read-only content. The squares without fill textures represent pages that require user input. We'll discuss shading and textures later in Chapter 6, "Illustrating Light, Motion, and Other Concepts." I used an inverted triangle to represent the starting point of the diagram. If you can draw the elements in Figure 2.22, you can draw a site map.

FIGURE 2.22

Journey Maps, Flow Charts, and Sequential Diagrams

Sequential diagrams can be used to map processes, journeys, and systems. In design, we use them to visualize journeys and tasks that are completed by users. Any journey, sequence, or process can be visualized using a sequential diagram.

We can use sequential diagrams to capture any process, even simple everyday processes. Let's start with a simple one. The photos in the next three figures loosely depict the process for preparing sweet potatoes. We usually start by rinsing the potatoes, as shown in Figure 2.23. We peel and chop the potatoes as suggested in Figure 2.24. Finally we coat in olive oil, season, and place them in the oven in Figure 2.25.

FIGURE 2.23

FIGURE 2.24

A process diagram as depicted in Figure 2.26 can be used to depict all the steps in this same process as depicted in Figures 2.23, 2.24, and 2.25.

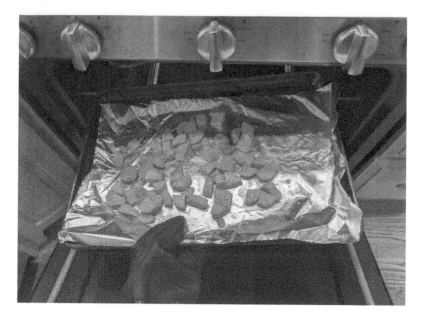

FIGURE 2.25

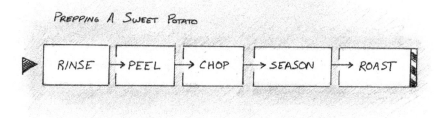

FIGURE 2.26

When we're redesigning a digital product, we usually start by mapping the current journeys in completing a task or achieving a goal within the app. The maps are then used to identify pain points in that journey. They highlight opportunities for removing or combining steps and eliminating people's pain points within the process. This map provides a guide for creating a new and improved journey that will provide direction for our product's redesign.

Going back to the fitness app we looked at a moment ago in Figure 2.21, let's map how an athlete might look up and modify details on a recent run automatically tracked by the fitness app. It might look something like the process diagram we see in Figure 2.27.

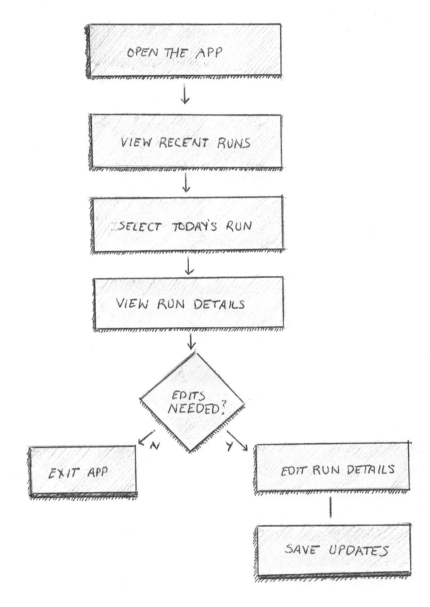

FIGURE 2.27

These diagrams are made up of boxes, arrows, repeating lines, and sometimes icons. A shape or symbol should be included to provide a clear starting point in this picture. The elements we used for this diagram are displayed in Figure 2.28.

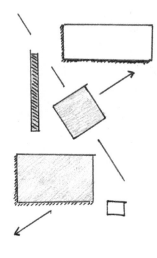

FIGURE 2.28

Mind Maps

Mind maps are a great way to organize information. Product design teams typically use them to organize ideas, thoughts, and research. These maps especially work well when organizing the information hierarchically because they resemble a tree-like structure. Figure 2.29 depicts an alternate representation of the mind map I created for Chapter 1. It maps and categorizes the benefits of drawing.

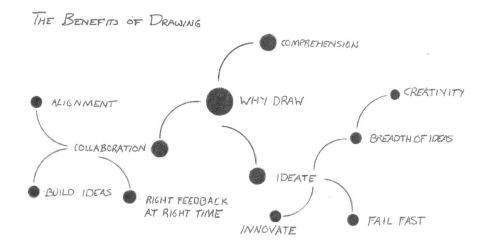

FIGURE 2.29

If you look at the mind map in Figure 2.30, you'll see that it is simply a cluster of points connected by lines. If you're not comfortable with drawing, points and lines are some of the easiest things to draw.

FIGURE 2.30

Digital Products, Screens, Interfaces, and Components

We often draw interfaces and screens that will be available in our new product. In Figure 2.31 you can see a few sample interface drawings. The drawing on the left likely represents a screen that's part of a mobile app. The drawing on the right represents a screen that is part of a desktop dashboard. At first glance, these drawings may seem complex. Can you break them down into their fundamental elements?

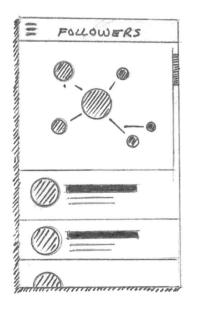

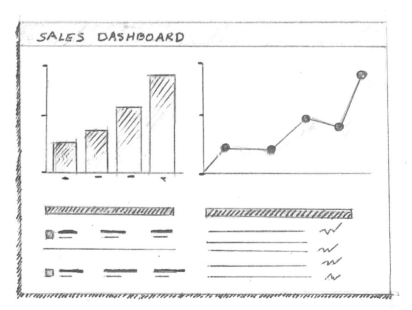

FIGURE 2.31

The basic shape containing the drawing mirrors the shape of the device's screen that will display our app. As highlighted in Figure 2.32, we typically use boxes to represent rectangular devices, and we use circles to represent other devices like watches.

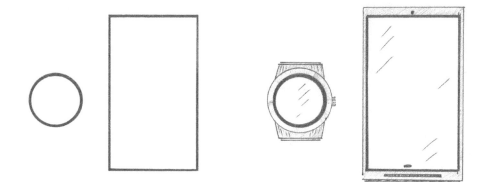

FIGURE 2.32

Interface elements within the screen layout are made up of basic shapes, points, and lines. Let's take a look at the examples in Figure 2.33. We can use thick lines to represent headlines. Blocks of thinner lines might represent text as depicted in the left and center drawings in Figure 2.33. Boxes with an X can be used to represent an image or icon as illustrated in the center drawing in Figure 2.33. Combinations of boxes are used to represent form inputs and buttons as depicted by the drawing on the right in Figure 2.33. We will cover more specifics in later chapters.

FIGURE 2.33

The collection of diagrams and drawings displayed in Figure 2.34 represent the majority of drawings you'll need to create with your team.

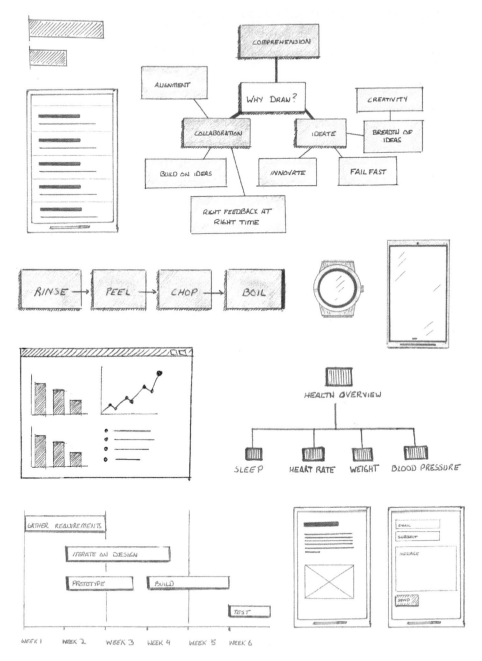

FIGURE 2.34

If we were to take inventory of all the shapes and elements we used in these drawings, you'll notice they have a lot in common. They can all be distilled down into the same set of basic shapes and lines displayed in Figure 2.35. Even with shading, some of the shapes in the figure are essentially a variation on a theme. These are the building blocks of your visual library.

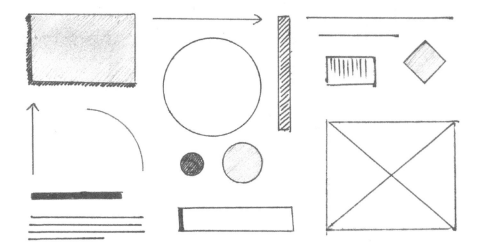

FIGURE 2.35

When you can distill a drawing down into these basic forms, you'll find that drawing is much more approachable, and you'll pick it up more quickly. You'll spend less time thinking about how to draw the picture and more about the idea it represents.

Next, let's take a closer look at the marks we make on the paper in order to draw these common elements.

CHAPTER THREE

LINES AND POINTS

Now that we've reviewed some common drawings and broken them apart into their basic shape elements, or building blocks, we're going to go a level deeper as metephorically illustrated in Figure 3.1.

Let's examine the lines and points we use to draw these shapes, be mindful of how these marks are constructed can make or break a drawing. Believe it or not, the very essence of your ideas and how they're perceived by your colleagues can be held within these marks.

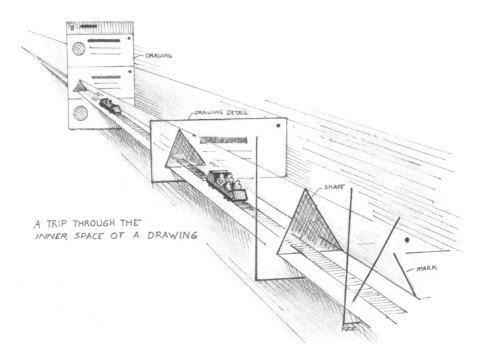

FIGURE 3.1

TELLING STORIES WITH LINES

Simple lines can be used to tell a rich story, and the way in which they're drawn can communicate a lot of information. Let's take a look at the drawing by Vincent Van Gogh in Figure 3.2.

FIGURE 3.2
Source: *Die Brücke von Arles*, Vincent Willem Van Gogh

When we first look at this image, we can see that he obviously used lines to draw the structural elements in the composition. This includes outlines of the stones and the wooden beams that make up the drawbridge. For this, he used straight lines. It's when we take a closer look at this drawing that we notice the more interesting applications of lines.

Notice how Van Gogh uses lines to represent the grass on the right river bank (Figure 3.3). The direction of the line implies the growth of the grass. The exaggerated nature of each line gives the grass an organic and overgrown feel.

Growing up, I spent a lot of time painting landscapes and scenes from nature. I always found water to be one of the most difficult materials to represent in a drawing or painting. Van Gogh's use of lines to represent water is just brilliant (Figure 3.4). The direction of the repeating lines implies a stillness in the water. His use of stacked lines also implies a reflection and a light source in the scene.

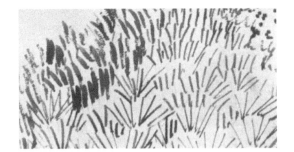

FIGURE 3.3

FIGURE 3.4

Finally, he used different line weights to represent light and shadows. Notice the diagonal cross braces that make up the underside of the drawbridge frame (Figure 3.5). The beams are represented with thicker lines, which implies that this portion of the bridge lies within a shadow.

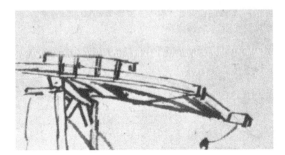

FIGURE 3.5

As you can see from this example, the possibilities are endless. The direction, speed, and pressure applied when we draw our lines can tell a lot about the ideas we're trying to develop and share. Let's take a look at a few ways in which you can draw different types of lines in your UX drawings.

Straight Lines

Like the stones and wooden beams in the aforementioned Van Gogh drawing, our screen-based interface drawings will feature a lot of structured, geometric elements as highlighted in Figure 3.6. When you're drawing these elements, line quality can make the difference between a bad drawing, a good drawing, and a great drawing.

Using clean lines will enable viewers of the drawing to focus on the idea it represents rather than how it was drawn. Lines should be drawn with a single quick stroke of the pen.

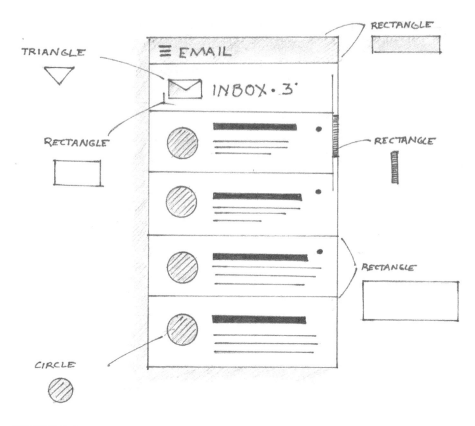

FIGURE 3.6

Because of this, there is no shame in using the proper tools, such as the straight edge pictured in Figure 3.7. If you don't have access to a ruler, triangle, or straight edge, you can even use the side of your smartphone. I've resorted to this while on the train, during my daily commute to New York City.

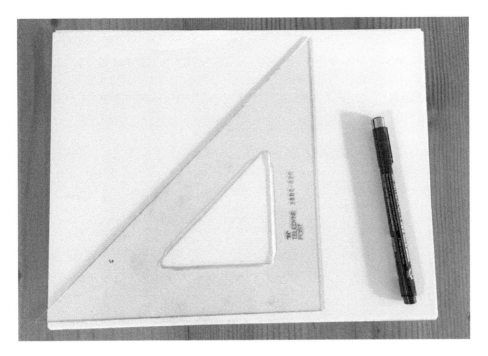

FIGURE 3.7

Remember, these are UX drawings. We're not trying to ace architecture school. It's okay to use tools. Poorly drawn shapes place extra cognitive load on a viewer. To prove this, let's do an A/B test with the sample sales dashboard drawing in Figure 3.8.

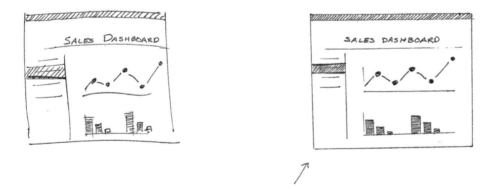

FIGURE 3.8

I drew the image on the left without a straightedge. I used a straightedge to draw the image on the right. I think we can all agree that the right image is much easier to read. It also has a more polished and professional look, which can inspire confidence in the author.

Circular Lines

Circles are one of the most difficult shapes to draw. There are several tools that will make your life easy here. For curved lines that will represent important structures and shapes, it doesn't hurt to use a protractor, compass, or circle template.

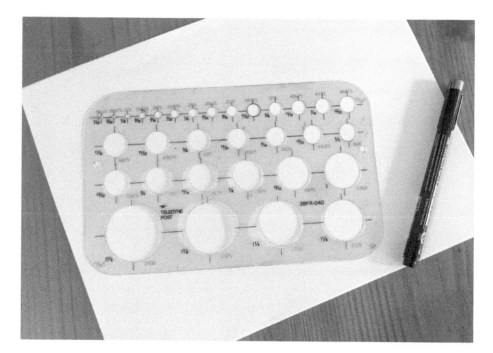

FIGURE 3.9

Take a look at the drawing of the watch face in Figure 3.10. The drawing on the left was drawn without a circle template. I used a circle template to draw the one on the right. Which is a clearer representation of a circular watch face?

I'm fairly certain that if you're designing an experience on a circular watch face, most of the UI elements will also be circular. All of the underlying lines used to create the drawing in Figure 3.11 were drawn with a circle template. Because of this, the visualization becomes the focal point of the drawing.

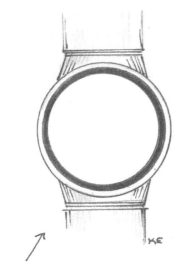

FIGURE 3.10

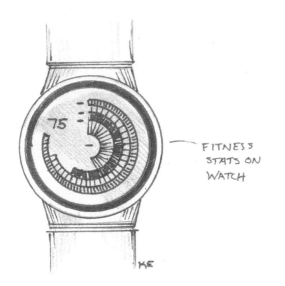

FITNESS
STATS ON
WATCH

FIGURE 3.11

Gestural Lines

Just like Vincent Van Gogh, we can use lines to suggest direction. It's
important to keep this in mind as you're drawing. When drawing a line, always
think about where the line would logically originate and start there. End the line
somewhere in the desired direction you want to go. Your line will most likely be
thicker at its origin than at its end. This will give your line a gestural quality that
implies direction and motion. It's a small detail that goes a long way in making
a drawing look polished.

To bring this to life, let's take a look at the example coming up in Figure 3.12. If you're drawing grass growing out of the ground, you can use lines to represent blades of grass. Since grass grows from the ground up, start your lines at the ground level and work upward. We can add a nice curvy, gestural quality to each line to give the grass a lively, organic feel.

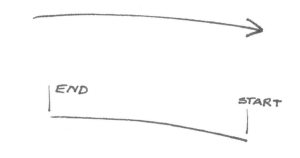

FIGURE 3.12

If you're drawing an arrow as depicted in Figure 3.13, start with the head end of the arrow. The arrowhead will be placed at the end of your line. The tail of the arrow will appear to trail off, giving it a nice gestural quality.

FIGURE 3.13

Here are a few other examples to consider: If you're drawing a tree diagram, the lines should start at each branch's origin and move outward. And if you're using lines to represent light, the radiating lines should start at the light's source and move outward, away from the source.

Line Weight

Just as Van Gogh used line weights to draw focus, you can do the same in your UX drawings. Thicker lines command more attention. You might use line thickness as a way to direct focus as suggested in Figure 3.14.

Let's take a look at an example in practice. In Figure 3.15, thick lines are used to create a focal point in the photos grid. This represents a photo that is selected for sharing.

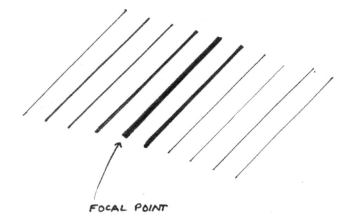

FIGURE 3.14

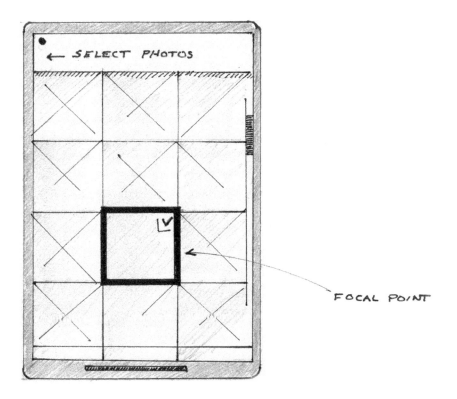

FIGURE 3.15

Finally, just like in the earlier Van Gogh example, lines can be used to represent concepts like light and shadow within a drawing, as shown in Figure 3.16. We'll cover more on shading techniques later on in Chapter 6, "Illustrating Light, Motion, and Other Concepts."

As you can see, lines play an essential role in describing the objects in our visual library. They can elevate the polish and quality of your drawing. Well-drawn lines can enable your colleagues to focus on the content of your drawings. These marks possess a lot of magical qualities, and the possibilities are exciting. When creating your next drawing, think about each line and what it represents.

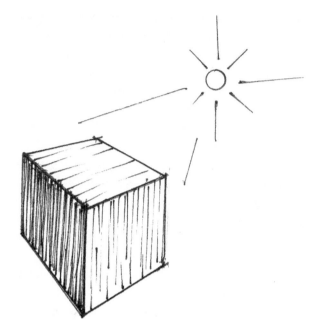

FIGURE 3.16

MAKING MEANING WITH POINTS

Points are the most basic marks we use in our drawings. They are a tiny part of a much larger image that carries meaning. In his book *Visual Grammar* (Princeton Architectural Press, 2006), Christian Leborg describes the point as something you cannot see or feel. It is a place without area and its position is defined by its x-, y-, and z-coordinates. When we're drawing, we use a basic dot to represent a point. We often get this when we first touch the pen to a drawing surface (Figure 3.17).

Simple points can carry a lot of meaning in our digital product drawings. To start, let's take a look at some of the drawings we already discussed in Chapter 2, "Reframing Our Thinking." To refresh your memory, take a look at the images in Figure 3.18 and Figure 3.19. These were some ways in which we represented the two values through an arrangement of points.

FIGURE 3.17

FIGURE 3.18

FIGURE 3.19

Points can be used to delineate marks in our interface drawings. In Figure 3.20, points were used to symbolize unread messages in the email inbox sketch.

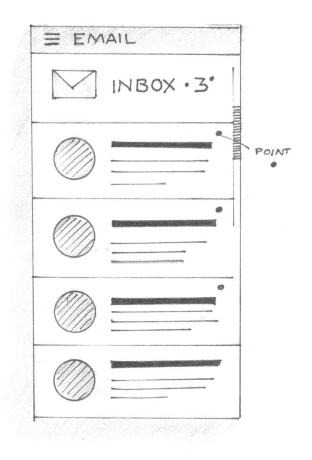

FIGURE 3.20

In Figure 3.21, the navigational element used in the image carousel was created by drawing a set of points.

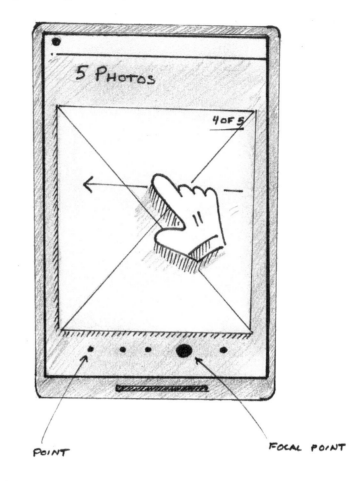

FIGURE 3.21

Just as we did with lines, we can use larger points to draw focus. Notice how the larger point in Figure 3.21 creates a focal point. In this case, the larger point, marked by the focal point label, indicates which photo we're looking at within the lineup of photos featured in the carousel.

Remember the mind map we reviewed in Chapter 2? Here's yet another version drawn with points (Figure 3.22). In this example, each point acts as a node and the diagram shows the relationships and connections between each node.

Figure 3.23 depicts how points can be used to represent the concept of light and shadows. I'll cover more on that later in Chapter 6.

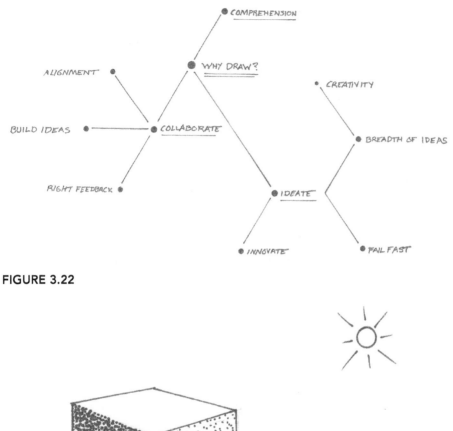

FIGURE 3.22

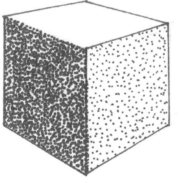

FIGURE 3.23

These are just a few examples of how points can be used in your product drawings. Just like lines, points are another versatile mark in our collection. Being mindful of how and when we use points in our drawings can really enhance the way in which we communicate our ideas.

TOOLS AND MATERIALS

Tools and materials also make a difference in the quality of our drawings. In addition to the aforementioned circle templates and straightedges, a good set of pens and pencils and the right paper are equally important.

For pens, I prefer Sakura's Pigma Micron pens. These are often sold in a set that includes multiple pens that can produce line weights of varying widths. The widths are measured in millimeters. This enables you to create thick lines for focal points and thinner lines for less important features. Medium pens can be used to create finer annotations and labels for your drawing. Some of the thin pens come in handy when creating shading and textures. Applying lines of varying thickness to your drawing will enable you to create drawings that look more polished and focused.

I also have a set of Faber-Castell graphite sketch pencils. I break them out when I'm creating higher quality drawings that I'll share with my colleagues. The degrees of softness of the graphite varies across the set. The harder pencils are nice for writing labels, annotations, and structural lines in the drawing. The softer pencils are nice for shading, creating focal points, and more gestural organic lines. The graphite also smudges nicely.

Finally, paper matters. Paper with more surface texture will enable you to create rougher, sketchier, and more ambiguous pencil lines. There are times when line ambiguity is key to communicating a feeling or the essence of your idea, as you learned from Professor Joe Biondo in Chapter 1, "Why Draw?" I'd suggest experimenting with pens, pencils, and various paper types to explore different styles. Then, find the right combination of tools and materials that works for you. It may take some time to do this, but it will make a difference, and it dramatically impacts the ways in which you make marks on the paper.

The way in which you draw your lines and points will affect people's focus, comprehension, and engagement with your drawing. Considerations like thickness, size, weight, and direction will enable you to start drawing with the finesse of a designer while enabling your shapes to carry rich meaning and allowing your greater drawing to convey a robust story about your idea.

Now, let's start using this knowledge to draw something. Let's start drawing some of the shapes, symbols, and elements that we'll reuse across all of our drawings. These are the elements of our visual library. We'll start building drawings out of rectangles, then we'll move on to other shapes like circles and triangles. We will also review some more complex symbols such as cursor hands and people.

CHAPTER FOUR

BUILDING FROM RECTANGLES

I claimed earlier that if you can draw boxes and arrows, you have what it takes to create a UX drawing—and a good one for that matter. Remember, in order to draw with your team, you don't have to be a critically acclaimed artist, nor do you have to be a designer. Let's start putting this claim to the test.

Think about what we covered in the previous chapter and find your straightedge. While you're at it, grab a pen or pencil and some paper. We're going to take an in-depth look at all of the most common elements you'll be using in your future product drawings. Let's start by drawing some lines to form a basic box (Figure 4.1). Your lines don't have to be perfectly level or parallel.

FIGURE 4.1

Next, let's draw an arrow. Just as we discussed in Chapter 3, "Lines and Points," think about the direction of the arrow and where to start and end your line (Figure 4.2).

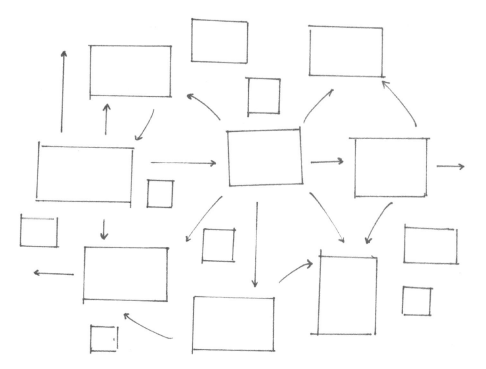

FIGURE 4.2

Fill up your paper with boxes and arrows so you become comfortable with this process. I included my own practice sheet in Figure 4.3. Now, let's see how we can use these shapes to create the basic building blocks of your visual language.

FIGURE 4.3

CREATING DIAGRAMS

As previously mentioned in Chapter 1, "Why Draw?," drawing can play an important role in helping you and your team synthesize the research by visualizing it. It can also help you plan the rest of your design process. It can enable you to align on requirements and a plan for execution. Let's take a look at how boxes can be used to create a few key diagrams that will supercharge your team's design process.

Process Diagrams

Boxes and arrows can be used to represent steps in a process diagram (Figure 4.4). They can be arranged in a stack or in a horizontal line. You can draw arrows to connect the boxes.

FIGURE 4.4

To make this diagram work, you can add labels that describe each step. I added a few very generic labels in Figure 4.5. You can also note information about the people and technology involved along the way. The entire diagram may represent a task or journey.

FIGURE 4.5

Remember the diagram that described the process for preparing and roasting a sweet potato in Chapter 2, "Reframing Our Thinking"? Figure 4.6 is an example of a more stylized version of a process diagram. It was drawn using the same shapes listed earlier. It just includes some extra symbols and shading to add visual interest. It's worth noting that *these extra accents and details are not essential in creating this diagram*.

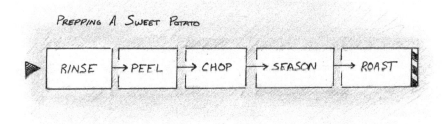

FIGURE 4.6

Now, let's try a version where we rotate one of the boxes 45 degrees to form a diamond (Figure 4.7). This typically represents a conditional, dependency, or decision point in a process diagram. You can even add a question mark for effect. Most process diagrams include conditions and dependencies.

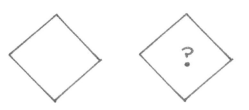

FIGURE 4.7

Figure 4.8 depicts how a conditional looks when added into a workflow diagram. Different combinations of boxes and arrows are used to create parallel paths that describe each outcome that occurs as a result of the options presented by the condition.

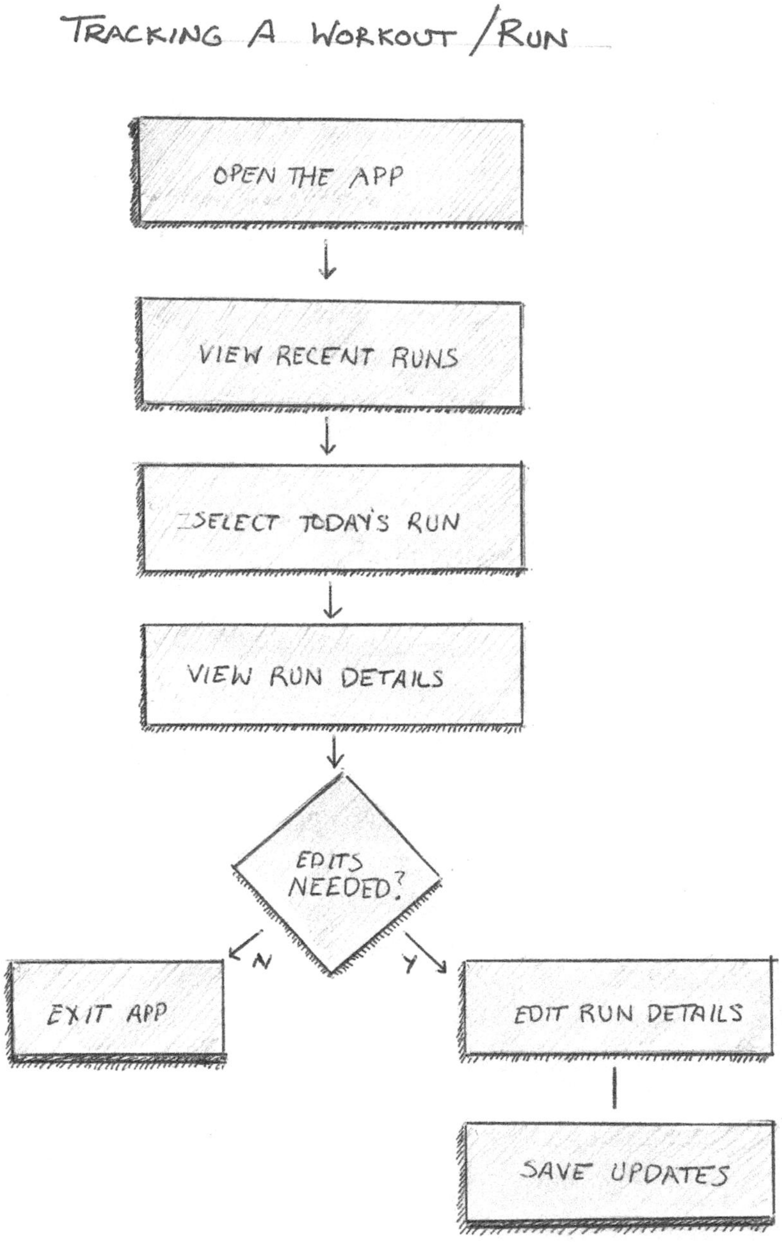

TRACKING A WORKOUT /RUN

OPEN THE APP

VIEW RECENT RUNS

SELECT TODAY'S RUN

VIEW RUN DETAILS

EDITS NEEDED?

N

EXIT APP

Y

EDIT RUN DETAILS

SAVE UPDATES

FIGURE 4.8

Tree Diagrams

Next, let's draw a cluster of boxes as illustrated in Figure 4.9. Start with a central box and work outward.

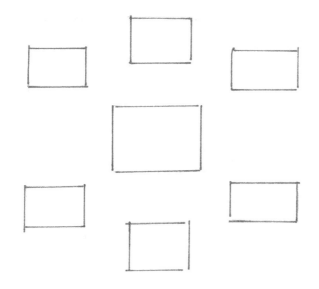

FIGURE 4.9

We can connect these boxes using arrows to create a tree diagram (Figure 4.10). Tree diagrams help us visualize hierarchical relationships. For example, they can be used to create a mind map to visualize organizational charts and nomenclatures.

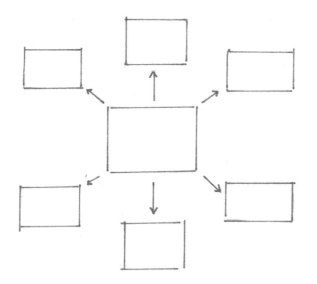

FIGURE 4.10

The mind map we discussed in Chapter 2 is a great example of a tree diagram as pictured in Figure 4.11. I used it to organize my thoughts on the benefits of drawing. In this case, I added some shading for effect, but you can see that boxes and connection lines are the primary two elements that make this diagram work.

THE BENEFITS OF DRAWING

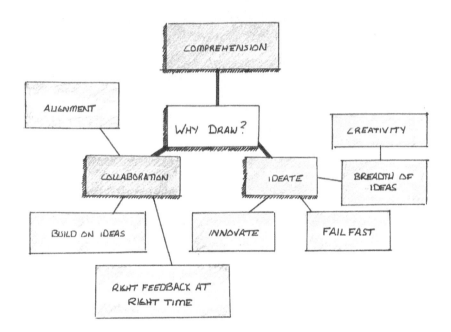

FIGURE 4.11

Let's try another arrangement of boxes. This time, let's arrange them in a pyramid form as drawn in Figure 4.12.

FIGURE 4.12

Next, let's connect them using dotted lines. The dotted lines will describe the hierarchical connections between the top row and the second row of boxes as illustrated in Figure 4.13

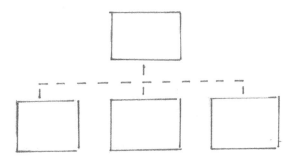

FIGURE 4.13

This is a good example of the structure used to create a site map or product map that details the information architecture of your website, products, or mobile app (Figure 4.14). Using these basic shapes, arranged in this structure, we can create something akin to the site map we reviewed in Chapter 2.

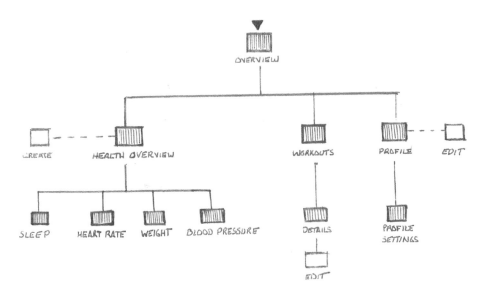

FIGURE 4.14

Network Visualizations

Finally, just to demonstrate the versatility of boxes, and to highlight the power of showing connections, let's revisit the radial arrangement of boxes used for our earlier tree diagram, as depicted in Figure 4.15.

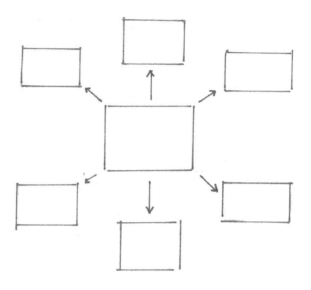

FIGURE 4.15

Now, to make a network visualization, let's reimagine the diagram's arrows. This same arrangement of boxes can be used to represent a network, as highlighted in Figure 4.16. Notice how the hierarchical relationships are removed yet we're still able to see the connections among the "networked" boxes. These types of diagrams can be used to show the relationships between people, processes, and technology within an organization.

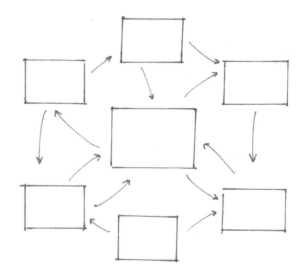

FIGURE 4.16

CONTENT ELEMENTS

At the time this book was written, user interfaces and digital content usually appeared on rectangular screens. As a result, a lot of the elements in our screen designs are based on monolithic, rectangular shapes. We can use boxes to represent a plethora of items.

Headline and Subheader Text

Let's start by reviewing ways to represent content. As drawn in Figure 4.17, a long, thin, filled box can represent a title, headline, subheader, or new chunk of content within your screen drawing. Using lines to represent text early on in the process will enable people to focus on your overarching idea, its architecture, and its value proposition. It'll enable them to focus less on the granular details like font choices.

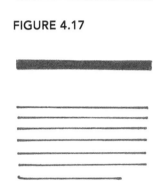

FIGURE 4.17

Content Blocks

By adding a few thinner parallel lines, as suggested in Figure 4.18, we can turn this into an iconic representation of a text block that includes a headline and a paragraph of body copy.

FIGURE 4.18

Image Placeholders

Let's draw an image placeholder like the one displayed in Figure 4.19. We'll start by drawing a box. Next, we'll place an **X** inside of it. Early on in the design process, it's okay if we're not sure what exactly the image will look like. This comes in handy when we're drawing content-heavy editorial website layouts.

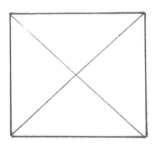

FIGURE 4.19

Lists

Let's combine the first three elements to represent a lockup with a thumbnail image and some supporting text as depicted in Figure 4.20. We can start with the image box. Then draw a thick line followed by a parallel thin line. This might represent an image thumbnail accompanied by text. UI elements like this are used in content recommendation panels, related content panels, and so on.

We can then stack this lockup layout to represent a list of content, articles, and pages to navigate to, as drawn in Figure 4.21

FIGURE 4.20

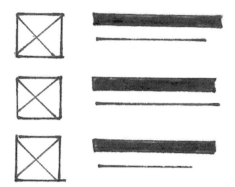

FIGURE 4.21

Content Layouts

The headline box, text lines, image box, and list can be combined in infinite ways to describe any number of page layouts. Let's try it out. We'll start by combining some of these elements to create a layout for a news website. We'll use a modified version of the text blocks from Figure 4.18, the image block from 4.19, and the lockup from Figure 4.20 to build a layout as illustrated in Figure 4.22.

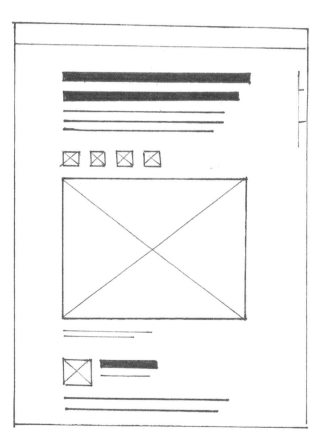

FIGURE 4.22

Since our elements are iconic in nature, we can add labels to our sketch to add more detail as highlighted in Figure 4.23. This is especially helpful for our teammates who are new to this process and aren't familiar with the visual language we're using to represent screen elements. I'll cover more on labels and annotations later in Chapter 8, "Using Flows to Tell Stories."

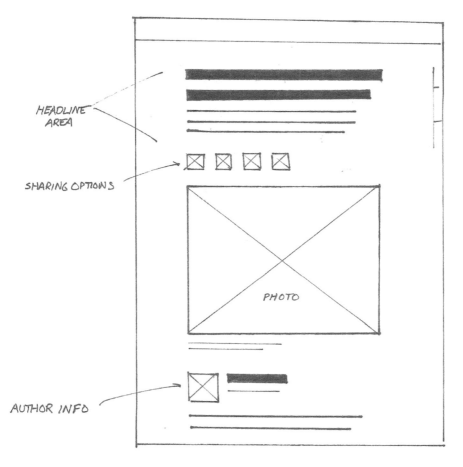

FIGURE 4.23

Figure 4.24 shows a side-by-side view of our drawing and the actual web page it's based on. Notice how the shapes in the drawing mimic the look of the key elements on the web page? The visual hierarchy is consistent. Prominent items such as the headline and image are the focal point of the drawing. I also used my set of Pigma Micron pens to draw this image. I used thicker points to draw the more important lines of each element, such as the headlines, the photo's bounding box, and so on. I used thin lines to draw the less important details within each element. This consideration for line weight and quality ensures that attention is drawn to the right areas of the sketch. It also gives it a more polished appearance. If you squint at the photo on the left in Figure 4.24, its elements start to look more like the elements of the sketch on the right.

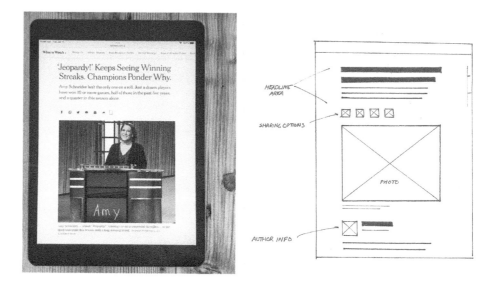

FIGURE 4.24

NAVIGATION ELEMENTS

Let's draw some screen navigation elements. Most of these items are built from boxes. We will review some common forms of navigation.

Lists

Let's start with a list screen. List screens are commonly found on most mobile apps, and their sole purpose is for navigation. Let's start by drawing a box with proportions similar to the box displayed in Figure 4.25

FIGURE 4.25

Now, let's stack a few of these boxes as suggested by Figure 4.26. It's okay if your lines aren't completely parallel and your angles aren't perfect. It adds to the character of the drawing and suggests the unfinished nature of the design. Worrying about geometric precisions will drastically slow down your process.

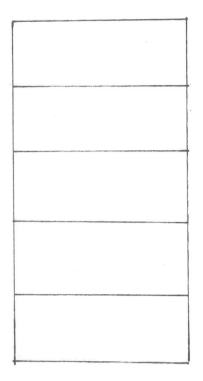

FIGURE 4.26

Inside each box, we can add a few elements. Let's reuse the photo and text lockup from Figure 4.20. List items in these layouts usually feature a thumbnail, icon, or symbol that describes the content within the list item. The result should look like Figure 4.27.

FIGURE 4.27

Finally, we'll add these details to the full stack of boxes as drawn in Figure 4.28. As this drawing takes shape, you might notice that it starts to look like a representation of a list screen.

This layout may seem familiar, as it is used by most popular email apps, including content recommendation engines, and music playlist screens. Figure 4.29 displays a side-by-side view of our list drawing and a Spotify playlist screen on a mobile device. While the Spotify screen has other UI elements, the list is the most prominent feature.

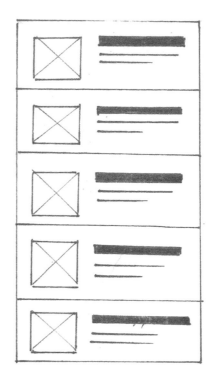

FIGURE 4.28

FIGURE 4.29

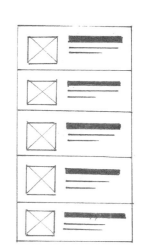

Tabs

Tabs are another common navigation element, especially on mobile devices.
Let's try drawing some navigation tabs. Let's start with a long and narrow
box as illustrated in Figure 4.30. This box will represent text. It's the same
element as covered in Figure 4.17.

FIGURE 4.30

Now, let's draw a few more of these filled boxes. They should share a
common baseline and appear on the same level, as depicted in Figure 4.31.

FIGURE 4.31

Next, place a box around the first filled box to show that the first tab
is active, as highlighted by Figure 4.32. This is one way to represent
navigation tabs.

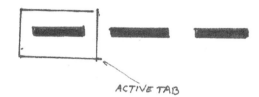

ACTIVE TAB

FIGURE 4.32

Navigational tabs are frequently used in mobile apps and appear toward
the bottom of the screen. That is because they are reachable by thumb
and can be operated by the same hand that is used to hold the device.
Figure 4.33 depicts the location of tabs within most mobile apps.

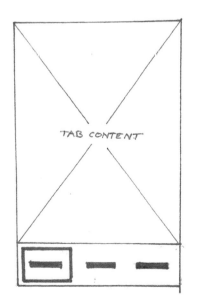

TAB CONTENT

FIGURE 4.33

Figure 4.34 highlights a real-world example of tabs in a mobile app. While it's common for tabs to appear at the bottom of the screen, they can appear anywhere. The example in Figure 4.34 consists of multiple tab sets. Tabs are a common UI element found on desktop and tablet apps as well. They're also a popular navigational element used in a lot of websites.

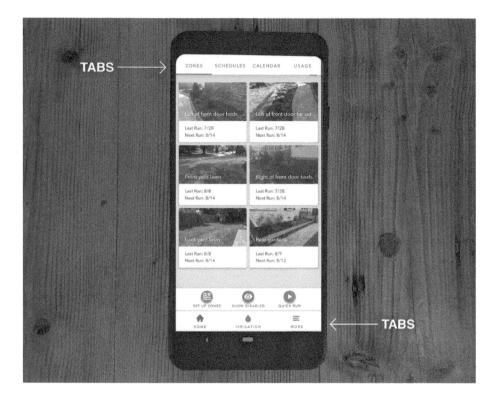

FIGURE 4.34

Breadcrumbs

FIGURE 4.35

This is one of the most useful navigation patterns, especially for websites with multiple levels of content. Next, let's try drawing a breadcrumb. Let's start by drawing a long box similar to the one in Figure 4.35.

Let's draw a few more similar boxes in a series. We will fill in the last box as depicted in Figure 4.36. The filled box represents the last page listed in the breadcrumb, which is the active page.

FIGURE 4.36

Finally, we'll add arrows between the boxes. This suggests the hierarchical relationships between the pages or levels symbolized by the boxes, as drawn in Figure 4.37.

FIGURE 4.37

You might also consider using a label instead of the filled box to indicate the active page, as written in Figure 4.38. This will provide an extra level of detail and context for your sketch, especially if it falls within a flow or series of sketches. Labeling is an important part of a sketch, and we'll cover more on labeling and annotations later in Chapter 8.

FIGURE 4.38

Breadcrumbs usually highlight the path we took to drill down through a set of web pages. Have you ever purchased a product from an online store? E-commerce sites usually provide breadcrumbs to help you navigate the taxonomy of products offered. Usually you select a product category, then a specific make and model based on a few key features you're interested in. Figure 4.39 shows where a breadcrumb usually fits into a web page's layout.

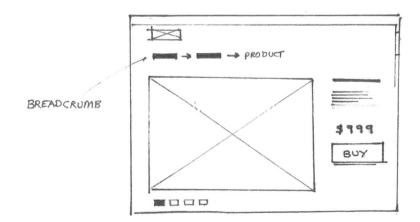

FIGURE 4.39

Grids

Finally, let's try one more. Most photo apps enable you to navigate collections of photos. To draw an interface like this, we'll start out by creating an image box (Figure 4.40)

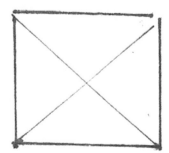

FIGURE 4.40

Next, let's combine a few of these boxes. We can start to build a grid. Figure 4.41 depicts an example of four photo boxes combined into a 2×2 grid.

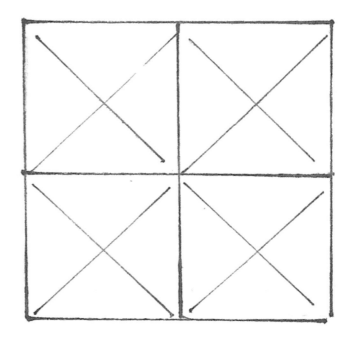

FIGURE 4.41

Finally, let's determine how many rows and columns we want to include in our photo grid. I chose a three-column layout (Figure 4.42). We can also create a focal point by drawing a thicker border around one of the photos to indicate that it has been selected.

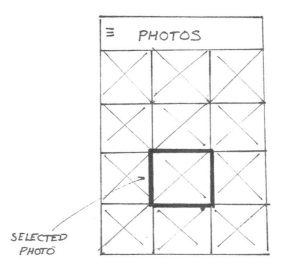

SELECTED PHOTO

FIGURE 4.42

In this case, I used two different pens to draw the grid. Since the vertical and horizontal nature of the grid's structure is more important than the diagonal accent lines, I used a thicker Pigma Micron pen to draw the vertical and horizontal lines. As a result, more emphasis is placed on the strong verticals and horizontal lines that make up this grid. In Figure 4.43, we see an example of an actual photos app. Our drawing provides a nice iconic representation of the elements in this screen.

FIGURE 4.43

FORMS

Web form inputs and controls are fairly universal. They're an integral part of most screen-based products and an essential part of any UX designer's toolkit. The majority of these elements can be built from rectangles. Let's take a look.

Text Fields

Let's draw a text input field. To do this, we will start by drawing a horizontal box as drawn in Figure 4.44.

FIGURE 4.44

Next we'll add a small vertical line just inside the box's left edge as depicted in Figure 4.45. For effect, you can turn that line into an I-beam.

FIGURE 4.45

Finally, we'll draw a long and narrow filled box above the text field box to represent the field's label, as illustrated in Figure 4.46.

FIGURE 4.46

Sometimes it's important to write out the actual text field's label. To do this, instead of placing a filled box above the text field, you can write in a label as depicted in Figure 4.47. Be sure to take your time and use clear handwriting to do this. We'll cover more techniques for adding labels in Chapter 8.

NAME

FIGURE 4.47

Text Areas

If we can draw text input fields, we can also draw text areas. This time we'll draw a larger, taller box, as shown in Figure 4.48.

FIGURE 4.48

Just as with the previous text field, we can add either a line or a handwritten label above the text area, the latter of which is highlighted in Figure 4.49.

MESSAGE

FIGURE 4.49

Checklists

Let's try a check box and checklist. For this, we will start with a square. Next, we'll draw a horizontal line to the right of our square as illustrated in Figure 4.50.

FIGURE 4.50

Finally, we'll place a check mark inside the box as displayed in Figure 4.51.

FIGURE 4.51

We can stack versions of this drawings to create a checklist. To make the checklist realistic, consider leaving some of the boxes unchecked, as illustrated in Figure 4.52.

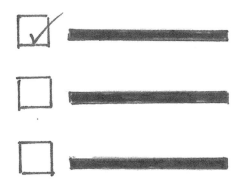

FIGURE 4.52

Buttons and Actions

FIGURE 4.53

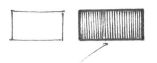

FIGURE 4.54

Most forms end with a button. To create this, we'll start by drawing a box. In this case, since we're creating a submit button, we'll write in the word *Submit*. Figure 4.53 depicts our hand-drawn box with the label inside it.

The drawing in its current state could easily be mistaken for a content card, text field, or another UI element. To mitigate this potential issue, we'll draw an affordance to indicate that this is an interactive button, as highlighted in Figure 4.54. To do this, we'll draw an inner border around the button's label.

In some cases, multiple buttons may appear in groups. In some forms, toast messages, alert bars, and dialogs, we may find a primary and secondary action. It's important to bring more focus to the primary action. To do this, you can use any number of techniques, such as using extra bold lines, or using hatching, fills, and shading as suggested in Figure 4.55.

FIGURE 4.55

Form Layout

Let's combine a few of our recent drawings to create a basic feedback form as drawn in Figure 4.56. The form will consist of a few text fields, one to capture the customer's name and another to capture the customer's email address. A large text area will provide a method for capturing the customer's detailed product review. Of course, we'll have to add a check box for accepting the terms of service. Finally, we'll add a prominent submit button at the bottom of the form. To provide additional detail, we will write out each form label instead of using a filled box.

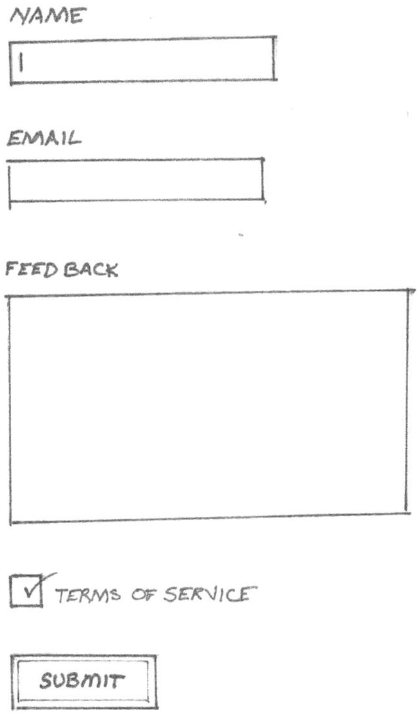

FIGURE 4.56

At this point, we're only scratching the surface. There are plenty of other form elements to consider. This initial set covers most form elements that can be drawn with boxes only. We will cover more options such as drop-down menus and radio groups later in the next chapter.

Charts and Graphs

Charts, graphs, and visualizations are included in nearly every app. Whether it's visualizations in a dashboard or a simple progress bar on a loading screen, there are several visualization elements that can be drawn with rectangles. Let's take a look.

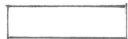

FIGURE 4.57

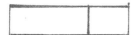

FIGURE 4.58

FIGURE 4.59

FIGURE 4.60

Progress Bars

Progress bars are used to show the progress of something. They can be used to show the load progress of an app, feature, or web page. They can be used to represent user ratings of a product, service, or experience. Progress indicators can show time remaining on a timed function and even your progress in completing a specific task like a workout. They can be drawn using two simple boxes. Let's start by drawing on a long and narrow box as depicted in Figure 4.57.

Next, we can draw a vertical line that cuts the box into two segments: one that's two-thirds of the box and one that's one-third, depicted in Figure 4.58.

Finally, let's fill in the first segment on the bar as illustrated in Figure 4.59. You might consider using a pencil for lighter shading, or you can use a hatching pattern with your pen. This will invoke the feeling that we're filling the box based on some sort of measurement.

Bar Charts and Histograms

Bar charts and histograms are useful visualizations that appear in most dashboard layouts. Bar charts are used for comparing categorical information based on a specified metric. Histograms are useful when showing changes over time. To draw a bar chart, let's start with the basic rectangle drawn in Figure 4.60. It should be tall and narrow. This will represent the first vertical bar on our chart.

Next, let's draw a set of vertical rectangles that run parallel to this first one, as depicted in Figure 4.61. The heights of these bars can vary; however, they should share a common baseline. I usually increase the height sequentially for effect—I'll explain why later on in Chapter 9, "Telling Engaging Stories." I think we can agree that this is starting to look more like a chart.

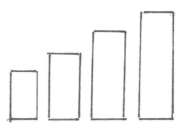

FIGURE 4.61

To take it a step further, we can draw a vertical line representing a y-axis to the left or right of the chart as displayed in Figure 4.62. It's up to you. The goal here is to symbolize that we're using the height bars to measure something.

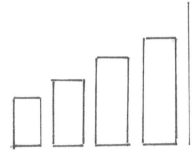

FIGURE 4.62

Finally, we can add small filled boxes that represent text labels beneath each bar, as depicted in Figure 4.63. If you'd like to provide additional context and detail, you can write in these labels. That's it! We have ourselves a chart.

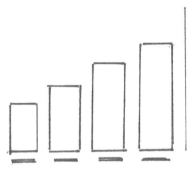

FIGURE 4.63

To draw a horizontal bar chart, we will do the same thing but with a different orientation. Instead of drawing vertically oriented bars, let's draw horizontally oriented bars. We will start with a single horizontal bar as depicted in Figure 4.64.

FIGURE 4.64

Next, we will add more horizontal bars, an x-axis line, and our labels, as illustrated in Figure 4.65. We'll follow the same basic steps we followed to draw the vertical bar chart, just in a different orientation. Horizontal bar charts are great where time is not a dimension.

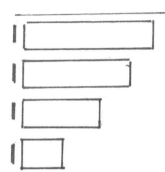

FIGURE 4.65

Let's revisit the vertical bar chart we already drew in Figure 4.63. We can divide the bars into segments to create a stacked bar chart as depicted in Figure 4.66. Stacked bar charts highlight differences in multiple categories.

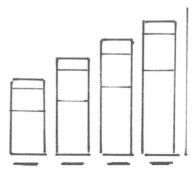

FIGURE 4.66

For effect, we can add shading for each of the segments, as depicted in Figure 4.67. For the bottom segment on each bar, let's add some hatching to create a sense of shading. We can use less dense hatching on the middle segments to represent a slightly lighter shade as shown in Figure 4.67.

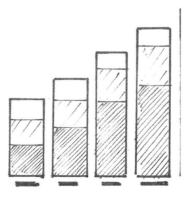

FIGURE 4.67

We can easily create a grouped bar chart by modifying the position of each bar along its x-axis as depicted in Figure 4.68. Grouped bar charts can be used to show comparisons over time. For example, in the figure, we can visualize revenue generated by a set of products for this past month as indicated by the darker bars. We can compare that to revenue generated by the same set of products for the previous year as indicated by the light bars. Each bar grouping represents a product in this case.

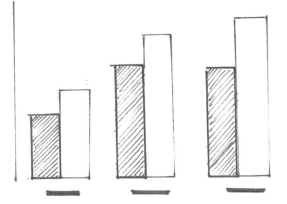

FIGURE 4.68

Line Charts and Area Charts

Line charts are an essential part of any dashboard. They enable us to visualize changes over time. They also enable us to compare many categories of continuous trends and patterns. It's one of the most common charts used in everyday dashboards. To draw a line chart, we'll start with a basic box as drawn in Figure 4.69.

FIGURE 4.69

We'll add a zigzag line inside the box to represent the chart type. For effect, I prefer to start my zigzag line in the bottom-left corner of the chart and end it in the upper-right corner as depicted in Figure 4.70. I usually do this unless I'm certain the data is supposed to trend in a different direction. Again, I'll explain more on my rationale in Chapter 9.

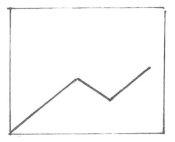

FIGURE 4.70

You can add points to the elbows of the zigzag for effect. These might suggest points where you can interact with the line to find out more information about the represented values, as highlighted in Figure 4.71.

You can take any line chart and add shading to convert it to an area chart. Figure 4.72 depicts a drawing of an area chart (left) and a stacked area chart (right) that were created using this technique.

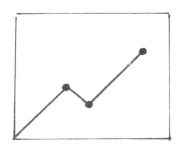

FIGURE 4.71

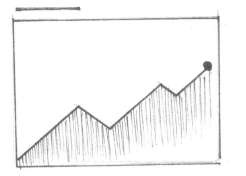
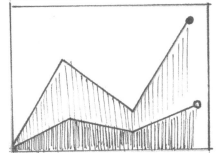

FIGURE 4.72

Dashboards

Next, let's arrange some of these chart drawings in order to create a simple dashboard. Your drawing might look like the sketch in Figure 4.73. Notice how I also integrated some navigation elements like tabs and written labels to provide more details about this dashboard's content.

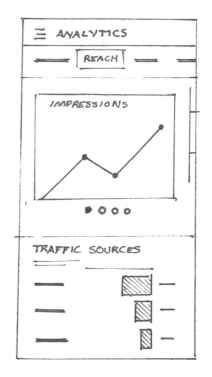

FIGURE 4.73

This is actually a sketch based on the YouTube Analytics dashboard, shown in Figure 4.74. You can see how the chart in the sketch does a nice job of symbolizing the chart in the actual dashboard. Again, all of these elements are iconic in their nature, and that's okay.

There are plenty of chart types that I didn't cover. There are several other charts that are built from boxes. Some examples include boxplots, waterfall charts, and treemaps. You'll use very similar methods for drawing each of them. In any case, it's important to start with the box shapes found in each chart, then layer in the supporting elements as you go. When it comes to charts, this is just the beginning. There are also plenty of other charts that are built from other shapes, which we'll explore in other sections of this book.

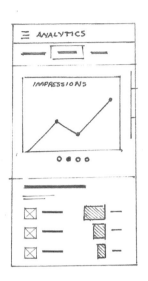

FIGURE 4.74

Interface Elements

In the spirit of providing a near-exhaustive list of elements, let's take a look at a few interface elements. Scroll bars, dialogs, and cards are commonly used in screen layouts. Let's jump in and take a closer look.

Scroll Bars

Scroll bars are a surprisingly important element in most sketches. They can be used to represent content-heavy modules, screens, and overlays where the content extends beyond the element's viewable area. This is a strong tool when explaining how your UI design might scale to accommodate more content. The scroll bar is a tall rectangle with one extra-long vertical line as depicted in Figure 4.75. For effect I added some shading to the scroll bar's handle.

FIGURE 4.75

Dialogs and Modals

Dialogs are popular UI elements used in a lot of screen-based products. They are used to provide contextual information and serve as a prompt to take action. They are usually smaller boxes that pop up over your screen. To draw one of these UI elements, you can start by drawing a box, then another box around it as depicted in Figure 4.76.

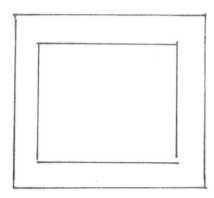

FIGURE 4.76

For added effect, we can add shading between the two boxes as illustrated in Figure 4.77. This places emphasis on the dialog itself. Let's add a primary and secondary button to the dialog.

FIGURE 4.77

Cards and Stacks

Are you feeling adventurous? Would you like to try something more advanced? In this book's preface, I shared a concept for an atomic force microscope UI (Figure 4.78). The design was based on a pile of stacked cards that represented an underlying workflow. Let's take a look at how we might draw the stack of cards.

Let's start by drawing a box with proportions like the box shown in Figure 4.79.

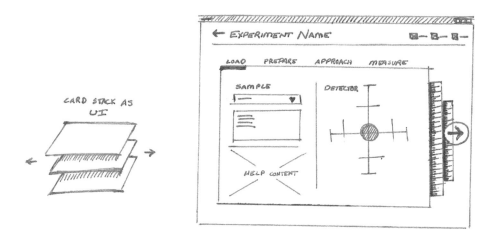

FIGURE 4.78

FIGURE 4.79

Next, we'll draw an *L* that runs along the left edge and bottom of the box. Offset the position to give the illusion of perspective, as drawn in Figure 4.80.

FIGURE 4.80

We will continue to repeat this step until we have a stack of cards as shown in Figure 4.81. The number of lines does not have to match the number of actual cards you'll anticipate featuring in your final design.

FIGURE 4.81

The position of our L-shaped lines should be offset as depicted in Figure 4.82.

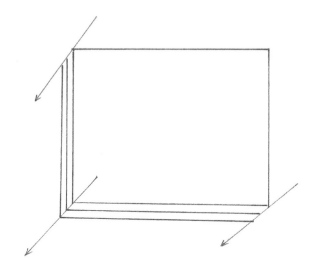

FIGURE 4.82

You can modify the position of the extra lines to give the illusion of different perspectives and views as highlighted in Figure 4.83. The existing perspective provides a worm's-eye view of the card set. We can move the lines to the top and left side for a bird's-eye view, as depicted in Figure 4.83.

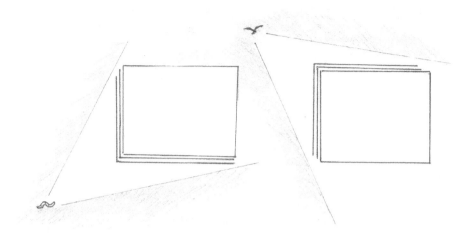

FIGURE 4.83

And there you have it. While this isn't an exhaustive list of elements drawn from boxes, it's a good start, and you'll likely use them in the vast majority of digital product drawings you create with your team. Now, in the next chapter, let's take a look at some other common elements built from other basic shapes.

CHAPTER FIVE

BUILDING FROM CIRCLES, TRIANGLES, AND MORE

While combining lines, boxes, and arrows goes a long way, you'll need to be able to draw elements based on other shapes, like circles and triangles. Once you master that, we'll explore some more complex forms like simple representations of people and cursor hands. Let's jump in.

CIRCULAR ELEMENTS

Let's start with a basic circle and a few elements we can build out of circles. Get your circle template or compass ready. Let's try drawing a bunch of circles similar to Figure 5.1. Feel free to use different sizes and fill up your paper.

Forms: Radio Groups

We'll start with the most utilitarian yet essential uses of the circle, and that's in forms. Circles are what separate a checklist from a radio group. Radio groups allow people to make only one selection within the group.

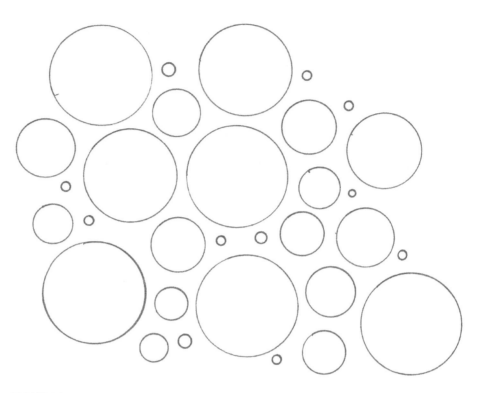

FIGURE 5.1

FIGURE 5.2

Remember how we drew the checklist? Instead of using squares and checks, let's use circles and points. Let's start with a basic circle as drawn in Figure 5.2. Let's draw a small circle that's approximately a quarter inch in diameter.

Next, just as we did with the check box, let's add a thick text line to the right of the radio button as depicted in Figure 5.3.

FIGURE 5.3

Radio buttons only make sense when they appear in a group, so let's draw a few more of these lockups in a stack as illustrated in Figure 5.4.

To finish off our radio group, we'll add a label and a preselected option by filling in one of the dots as depicted in Figure 5.5. A radio group enables you to select one item within the group. A good example of this is when you're ordering a product online and choosing a shipping option. You can select only one shipping method.

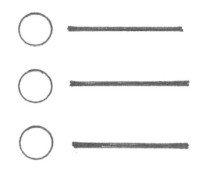

FIGURE 5.4

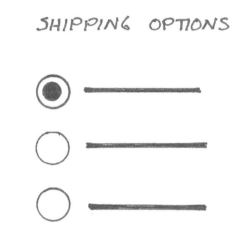

FIGURE 5.5

The Circle as a Symbol

Circles are an important element in human culture and have been a metaphor embraced by virtually every civilization that has ever existed (Lima, 2017). Important in nature and city layouts and a metaphor for a community, it's not going away anytime soon. Given its importance as a symbol, you can bet that it still remains as a key visual in today's technologically advanced society. Now, without further ado, let's jump in and explore the powerful symbolism that comes with a circle.

Status Icons

You can place any number of symbols inside a circle to create an icon. Let's start with the circle itself, as drawn in Figure 5.6.

FIGURE 5.6

You can add any type of character in the middle of the circle to create an icon, as depicted in Figure 5.7. An exclamation point might represent a warning or an alert. An **X** can represent a failure or error. Check marks might represent a positive or completed status. Flip the exclamation point upside down to create a lowercase *I* and we have ourselves an information icon. The possibilities are endless. Since the majority of drawings consist of many boxes and angular forms, the curved nature of the circle will draw attention, which is why this is a good form to combine with a status icon.

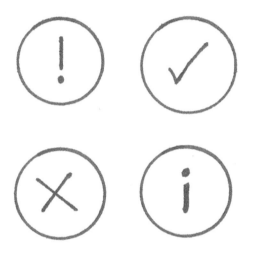

FIGURE 5.7

Time Icon

Let's use a circle to represent time. For this, we'll draw a classic representation of an analog clock with two hands. This symbol has carried its meaning for hundreds of years. Let's start by drawing a circle as sketched in Figure 5.8.

In order to draw a clock, start with the origin or center point of the circle. Draw two hands, one longer than the other as drawn in Figure 5.9. You can draw them in any direction you prefer to represent a desired time.

Emojis

At the end of the day, other people are going to use the products we're designing. In some cases, it's important to be able to express their emotion, whether it's when mapping the ways in which they use an existing product or mapping an emotional curve in a research presentation. Circles are a great starting point for creating emojis, as drawn in Figure 5.10. Let's start with a basic circle. For this exercise, it helps to keep the circle small.

By adding two points and a few curved lines, we can express a range of emotions through drawing. This enables us to bring a human element into our drawing. Check out the collection of emojis in Figure 5.11. This covers a range

FIGURE 5.8

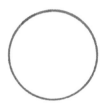

FIGURE 5.9

FIGURE 5.10

of emotions. I even threw in a few extras for fun. Try drawing a few of these expressions yourself.

FIGURE 5.11

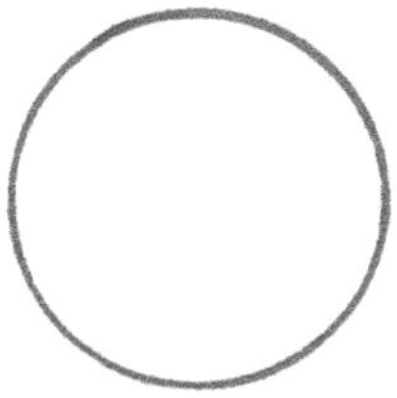

FIGURE 5.12

Profile Icons

Let's draw another commonly used icon. This can be used to represent avatars and profile images. You can even use it to represent people in a process diagram or org chart. Once again, we'll start with a simple circle as depicted in Figure 5.12.

Next, we'll add another circle inside the first circle. It should be centered horizontally, but it can appear in a slightly offset location as depicted in Figure 5.13.

FIGURE 5.13

We can draw two lines to form the shoulder lines that will connect the inner circle to the outer circle, as illustrated in Figure 5.14.

Finally, we'll bring this all together by filling in lines as depicted in Figure 5.15.

We can use multiples of the drawing in Figure 5.15 to represent a community as depicted in Figure 5.16. We can use this metaphor to represent user groups, online communities, and teams within an organization.

FIGURE 5.14

Charts

You can also include various types of charts to convey information. The following sections describe some of the options.

FIGURE 5.15

Pie Charts

Let's try drawing a pie chart. Pie charts are great for showing part-to-whole relationships. They enable us to visualize how the parts of something make up its whole. Invented in the beginning of the nineteenth century, this chart still remains a staple in most modern dashboards. Love it or hate it, it's here to stay. Let's build a pie chart out of a circle. We'll begin by drawing another circle, as illustrated in Figure 5.17.

FIGURE 5.16

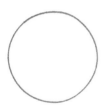

FIGURE 5.17

FIGURE 5.18

FIGURE 5.19

FIGURE 5.20

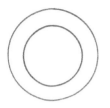

FIGURE 5.21

FIGURE 5.22

Inside your circle, mark a point at the circle's origin as highlighted in Figure 5.18. It's best to use a pencil for this since the pencil mark can be erased.

Next, we'll draw lines that extend from the circle's origin to its border as depicted in Figure 5.19. Moving in a clockwise direction, I start with my largest slice and work down from there. The result is an iconic and more readable pie chart drawing. Of course in real life, this might not be the case. We'll discuss how to adapt your drawings to account for real-world scenarios, constraints, and data in Chapter 9, "Telling Engaging Stories."

Finally, for effect we can use shading to fill in a specific slice of the pie as depicted in Figure 5.20. This is optional, and we'll discuss shading techniques later in Chapter 6, "Illustrating Light, Motion, and Other Concepts." In case you're interested, I used both pencil and pen to create this textured fill.

Donut Charts

One of my favorite versions of variations of the pie chart is the donut chart. You can use the space in the empty, inner circle of the donut to highlight key metrics. Let's revisit the circle from Figure 5.17. Then, let's draw an inner circle. You can use the guides on your circle template to properly line up the inner circle. The goal is to create two concentric circles on your paper as drawn in Figure 5.21.

Next, we can draw dividing lines to form two segments. We can fill in one of the segments as depicted in Figure 5.22.

Finally, let's leverage our reason for using a donut chart by using the empty space in the middle of the donut. In this drawing, let's highlight the metric displayed in the chart as depicted in Figure 5.23.

FIGURE 5.23

Scatterplots

Now we will create a basic scatterplot chart. Scatterplots help us visualize a comparison between two variables. Once again, let's start by drawing a small circle about a quarter inch in diameter as depicted in Figure 5.24.

FIGURE 5.24

We can draw a few other circles in a cluster. For this drawing, my cluster of circles will run from left to right and from bottom to top as depicted in Figure 5.25.

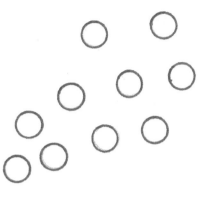

FIGURE 5.25

Next, let's draw an x- and y-axis using a straightedge, as drawn in Figure 5.26.

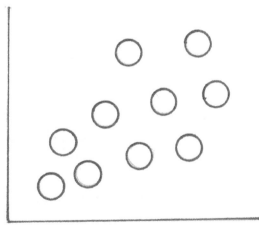

FIGURE 5.26

Finally, we can fill in the dots for effect as depicted in Figure 5.27. There we have it. A scatterplot!

Bubble Charts

Let's take the scatterplot a step further. Bubble charts enable us to compare three variables. Each plot's size can be based on the value of the third metric. The plots begin to look like bubbles, hence the name bubble chart.

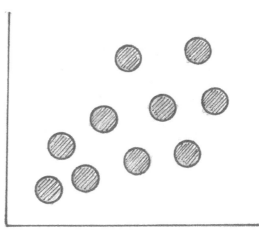

FIGURE 5.27

Hans Rosling created a famous bubble chart that shows the correlation between a country's income per person and life expectancy. These two variables are measured on the x- and y-axis, respectively. In this chart, Hans introduced a third variable, which is each country's population. He used the size of each country's bubble to represent its population. At the time this book was written, you could view this visualization at gapminder.org.

If you end up drawing one of these, be prepared to describe what the size of the bubble represents. To draw the bubble chart, we'll follow the same steps we followed to draw the scatterplot; however, we'll use different size circles as shown in Figure 5.28.

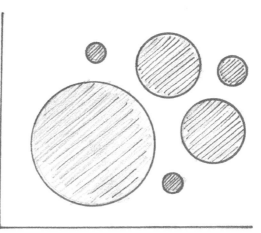

FIGURE 5.28

These are just a few elements that can be built from circles. These elements are yet another set of building blocks to add to your kit.

It's important to keep in mind that not all screens are rectangular. Take a look at the Nest Learning Thermostat in Figure 5.29. Notice how the visualizations and user interface are all based on circles.

FIGURE 5.29

The interface on the thermostat is based on circles. The process for drawing this would be nearly identical to the one we used to draw the donut chart in Figures 5.21, 5.22, and 5.23. Why not try it out? Grab your pen and paper and try to draw the elements on the thermostat's display. As mentioned in Chapter 2, "Reframing Our Thinking," some wearables like watches have circular screens. It's important to keep in mind that several watch screen elements can be built from circles, like the graphs depicted in the concept sketch in Figure 5.30. There are plenty of other screens that are circular in shape, and as we move into the future, circular screens will become more and more commonplace in our lives.

TRIANGULAR ELEMENTS

The triangle is one of my all-time favorite shapes. It is a symbol of strength and resilience. It's also used in many structures because it is revered as the strongest shape in nature.

Let's see how triangles can be used in our digital product drawings—starting with Figure 5.31.

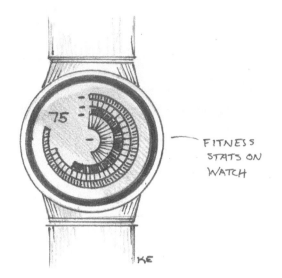

FIGURE 5.30

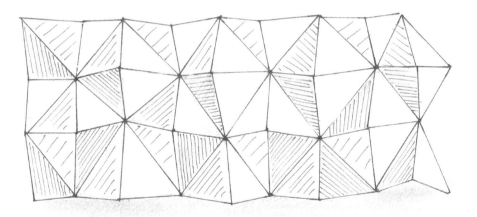

FIGURE 5.31

Navigation Controls

In the following sections, we will look at the options for including navigation controls.

Expand/Collapse Controls

To draw an expand/collapse control, draw a small triangle that points up. Draw another one that points down. Now we have ourselves an expand/collapse control as drawn in Figure 5.32

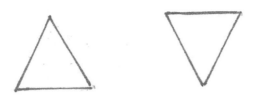

FIGURE 5.32

As we did with some of our earlier drawings, we might consider filling in the arrow, because it could be an indicator of something we can interact with on the screen (Figure 5.33).

FIGURE 5.33

Forward/Backward Arrows

To create a navigational arrow, we can turn our triangles on their sides and point them to the right or left as depicted in Figure 5.34.

FIGURE 5.34

Icons: Alerts, Warnings, and Anomalies

Here, we will look at various icons you can create. To create an alert icon, we'll draw a slightly larger triangle, as shown in Figure 5.35.

Next, we'll place an exclamation point in the middle of it, as drawn in Figure 5.36.

Just for fun, let's add a few small accent lines outside of the triangle to symbolize the urgency of the alert, as drawn in Figure 5.37.

FIGURE 5.35

FIGURE 5.36

FIGURE 5.37

Forms: Drop-Down Menus

Finally, let's draw a drop-down menu. To do this, we can draw an inverted triangle and a baseline that represents the field. The triangle should appear at the right end of the baseline as illustrated in Figure 5.38.

FIGURE 5.38

An alternate way to represent a drop-down is by placing the arrow inside a box as drawn in Figure 5.39.

FIGURE 5.39

I think it's safe to say that we're building out a robust library of common elements. So far we covered various screen elements built from circles and triangles. Next, feel free to look at some of your favorite apps and devices. Look at their screens. See if you can distill their elements down into some of these basic shapes and draw them. You can use the symbols and drawings we've already covered in this chapter.

ADVANCED ICONS AND SYMBOLS

It's time to start drawing some complex shapes and forms that you'll commonly use in your digital product drawings. This section is all about icons like the ones depicted in Figure 5.40. Some of these forms will help you describe ways in which people will interact with your product, others will focus on people themselves, the centerpiece of all of our product design work. Others will be used to enhance existing charts, graphs, maps, and visualizations we previously covered. Let's jump in!

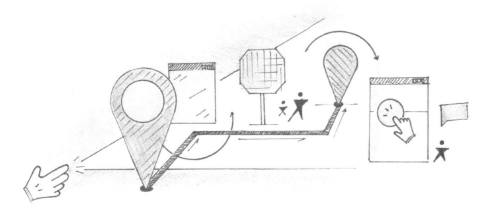

FIGURE 5.40

Octagons and Stop Signs

Let's grab a *pencil* and draw a square as depicted in Figure 5.41. Be sure to draw lightly as we'll eventually erase these pencil lines.

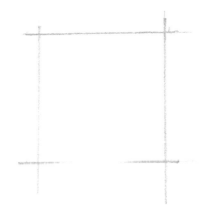

FIGURE 5.41

Now, draw diagonal lines cutting off each of the corners of the square as illustrated in Figure 5.42.

Next, trace the resulting shape with a pen, then erase the pencil lines as depicted in Figure 5.43. You should be left with an octagon. It's okay if the shape isn't perfect. As long as it reads as an octagon, it's a success.

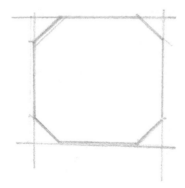

FIGURE 5.42

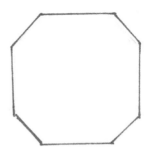

FIGURE 5.43

Now you have an octagon. You can add any number of icons and accents to this shape. For example, this can be used to represent the end of a process diagram. It can also be used to represent an alert. In Figure 5.44, I turned the octagon into a stop sign.

FIGURE 5.44

Location Markers

If you're not good at drawing maps, that's okay. We can use a placeholder icon to represent the concept of a location. To do this, we might simply draw an upside-down teardrop. Let's grab a circle template and get started. First, we'll draw the upper 60 percent of the circle, as depicted in Figure 5.45.

FIGURE 5.45

Next, we'll connect the open-ended portion of the circle by adding two straight lines that point downward, connecting to form a V shape as drawn in Figure 5.46.

FIGURE 5.46

Finally, we can add other accents, such as an inner circle for effect as illustrated in Figure 5.47. This isn't required, but it may fortify the meaning of the symbol.

FIGURE 5.47

People

People can be one of the most intimidating things to draw. When we're creating a new product, however, people are what matter most, especially if you work on a user experience team. Arguably, this is one of the most important elements in your visual language. There are several ways in which we can represent people without having to draw a perfect anatomically correct human body. Let's take a look.

FIGURE 5.48

FIGURE 5.49

One abstract yet elegant way to represent a person is as follows. Let's start by drawing a hump or upside down letter *U* as depicted in Figure 5.48.

Next, we'll connect the bottom of the hump with a slightly curved horizontal line as drawn in Figure 5.49.

After that, we'll add a circle above the existing drawing as displayed in Figure 5.50.

FIGURE 5.50

Finally, we can add some shading to draw attention to our icon. I chose a simple hatching pattern as depicted in Figure 5.51. I'll share more on shading later in Chapter 6.

FIGURE 5.51

The resulting drawing may look more like a board game piece than a human but it's enough to get the point across. In fact, a lot of the people icons found in our favorite mobile apps look like this. The example in Figure 5.52 depicts how people might be represented in a workflow diagram.

FIGURE 5.52

In this scenario, the people icons used in the fourth step of this workflow diagram represent a process step that is completed in person and not within an app screen like the other steps.

Another way to draw people is by drawing a partial star shape. Make sure the top point of the star does not cross the horizontal connector line of the next highest two points. Use Figure 5.53 as a reference when creating the semi-star shape.

FIGURE 5.53

Next, let's add a circle in place of the missing point, as drawn in Figure 5.54.

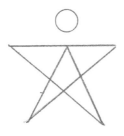

FIGURE 5.54

We can fill in the shape for effect (Figure 5.55). This drawing will look like a stylized stick figure.

FIGURE 5.55

Finally, Figure 5.56 depicts how this version of the icon might look in a process diagram. In this case we're using the icons to show people completing the fourth step, which takes place offline.

FIGURE 5.56

REPRESENTING INTERACTIONS

In nearly all cases, it's important to represent a method for interaction and input. This is especially true when drawing a flow of screens that represents the steps a person takes to complete a task or to achieve a goal when using your product. Let's start with the most difficult drawing. Then we'll fall back on a few easier alternatives.

Pointer Hands and Cursors

FIGURE 5.57

FIGURE 5.58

Hands are arguably the most difficult thing to draw. I've been drawing and painting since I was five years old, and I still struggle with drawing hands. To this day I don't know how I made it through my life drawing class in design school. Anyway, hands can be used to represent gestures and touch events on a mobile device. They can also be used to represent the click state of a mouse cursor. Let's take a look at how to represent a basic hand. Hands are simply a series of connected humps. Assuming we're drawing a right hand, the thumb should point in a northwest direction as drawn in Figure 5.57.

Now, let's draw the pointer finger. The pointer finger should be the longest finger and should point to the north, as depicted in Figure 5.58.

Next, add three small humps representing the remaining fingers. They should point in the same direction as the pointer finger, and they should be considerably shorter as drawn in Figure 5.59.

Finally, add a line that runs down to the wrist, representing the right side of the hand. You can even extend the line beneath the thumb downward if you wish, as illustrated in Figure 5.60

FIGURE 5.59

FIGURE 5.60

Now let's have some fun. Note the extra details added to the drawing in Figure 5.61. Let's add two accent lines to make them look like Mickey Mouse hands. This is something I always do for fun, and you'd be surprised at how many people picked up on this in the past and commented on it.

FIGURE 5.61

Click Interactions

Starting with our previous drawing, we can add other accents that further describe the interaction. We can add three radiating accent lines to represent a click or selection state, as drawn in Figure 5.62. For effect, I also added a drop-shadow to this hand, since it will appear to float over all of the screen elements.

FIGURE 5.62

Gestural Interactions

Let's revisit the hand drawing from Figure 5.61. Aside from adding a few embellishments like a drop shadow, we can add an arrow to suggest a swipe gesture, as displayed in Figure 5.63. The possibilities are endless.

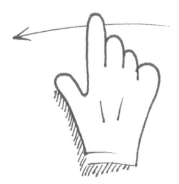

FIGURE 5.63

Describing interactions is an essential part of any digital product drawing. It helps your colleagues understand how people will interact with your product. Let's revisit the telemedicine app concept I shared earlier in this book (Figure 5.64). Notice how the hand icon explains the video player's behavior when the screen is scrolling.

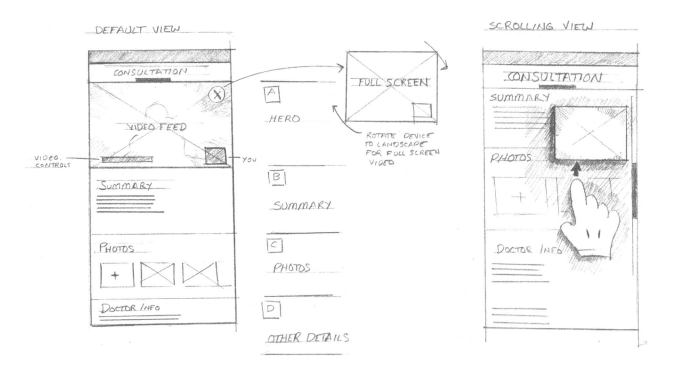

FIGURE 5.64

Alternatives for Drawing Gestures

So how did your hand drawings turn out? It'll probably take some practice to master. Here's a backup option for drawing gestures and mouse interactions. We can replace the hand with a filled dot as depicted in Figure 5.65. The same radiating accent lines and arrows will suggest the same click and swipe interactions as in our previous hand drawing.

FIGURE 5.65

CHAPTER SIX

ILLUSTRATING LIGHT, MOTION, AND OTHER CONCEPTS

Sometimes it takes more than the basic icons and symbols covered in the last two chapters to communicate the essence of an idea. Illustrating concepts like light, depth, form, material, motion, and texture can further explain your idea (see Figure 6.1).

There are a few simple ways to convey these concepts in your product drawings without having to have the skill or training of an accomplished artist. Let's take a closer look.

SHADING TECHNIQUES

Before we dive into the actual concepts, let's talk about shading. You can use different shading techniques to communicate many of the concepts explained in this chapter. Take a look at the drawing in Figure 6.2. In it, we can see how Leonardo da Vinci created a sense of light through the use of shading to help his viewers understand the complexities of this polyhedron form.

The drawing's light source originates from the top-left corner of the drawing. He used darker shading to represent surfaces that face farther away from the light source. Da Vinci's use of shading also gives us an increased sense of the polyhedron's material, shape, and texture.

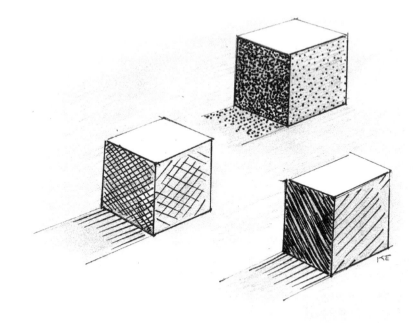

FIGURE 6.1

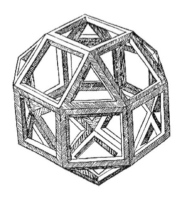

FIGURE 6.2
Source: Polyhedra by Leonardo da Vinci, from Luca Pacioli's *"De divina proportione,"* 1509 edition

Now let's do a deep dive into shading. We will examine how shading can be used to suggest concepts like light, elevation, depth, texture, focus, and more. There are many different techniques that can be used to create shading in a drawing. Figure 6.3 highlights a few popular ones. Pointillism, hatching, crosshatching, contour shading, and scribbling are all popular techniques. We can differentiate these techniques by looking at the marks we make on the paper to create them.

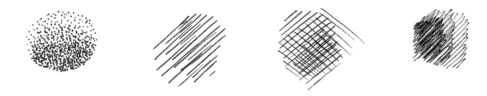

FIGURE 6.3

Most of these techniques consist of lines, points, or both. Pointillism relies on a collection of points to create a shade, while the remaining techniques rely on lines to create the shade. The density of these marks determine how light or dark the shade appears. We will take a look at each of these techniques in more detail as we introduce and explore the concept of lighting later in this chapter.

USING ACCENT MARKS

Let's revisit our knowledge of basic marks like the points and lines discussed in Chapter 3, "Lines and Points." We can add some stylized versions of these marks to our product drawings to convey concepts like elevation, sound, motion, luminance, and texture. Figure 6.4 highlights a few examples of this.

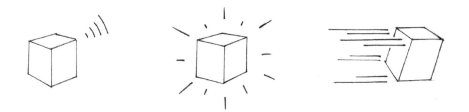

FIGURE 6.4

Now, let's take a look at how shading techniques and accent marks can be used to communicate several common yet abstract concepts.

LOOKING AT LIGHTING

This is one of my favorite concepts, and understanding the basics of lighting will help you better communicate the related concepts we'll review later in this chapter. To create a light source in our drawings, we can use the various aforementioned shading techniques to illustrate the shadows.

Pointillism

Many classic paintings were created using pointillism, a technique in which painted dots in distinct patterns were used to create the larger picture. Paul Signac's painting depicted in Figure 6.5 is a textbook example of pointillism.

FIGURE 6.5
Source: *The Port of Saint-Tropez,* Paul Signac 1901, oil on canvas, National Museum of Western Art, Tokyo

In this example, he uses a set of points in lieu of lines to create every element in the scene, including the boats and buildings. He also used it to describe the water, light, and the various textures within the painting. Pointillism, while somewhat tedious, is an effective way to create shadows that suggest a light source.

As you can see from Signac's painting, when there is a higher concentration of dots, the shadow appears darker. Notice the cube drawing in Figure 6.6. If our light source appears to the top right of the cube, the sides that face away appear darker.

Side 1 is the lightest. Side 2 is slightly darker since it doesn't directly face the light source. Side 3 is completely opposite of the light source and faces away from it. This is the darkest side, therefore it contains the highest concentration of points.

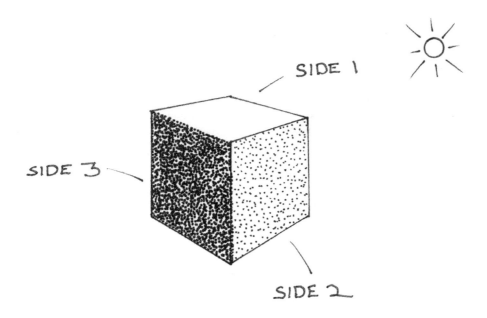

FIGURE 6.6

To make this more realistic, we can use a few points to suggest a cast shadow coming off of the darkest side of the cube, as depicted in Figure 6.7. This will give the object some visual weight and grounding, thus making the light source appear a bit more believable.

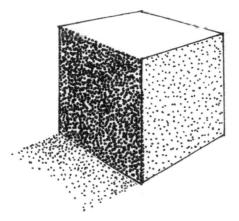

FIGURE 6.7

FIGURE 6.8

In Figure 6.8, we're applying pointillism to a sphere. Notice how the shading follows the curvature of the spherical form. We can create a gradient effect by slowly increasing the amount of points and their proximity to each other as we move away from the light source toward the lower left of the sphere, as depicted in Figure 6.8.

Go ahead and give it a try. Draw a few cubes and spheres. You can even trace the sample cube in this book and then shade it. Once you've practiced this technique a few times, we'll move on to some other shading techniques.

Hatching

Hatching is the use of lines to create shading. As with pointillism, the higher the concentration of lines, the darker the shading appears. Let's revisit our cube example in Figure 6.9. Again, notice how the hatching becomes denser on the sides of the cube that face farther away from the light source.

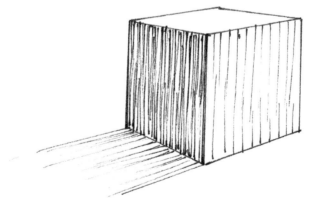

FIGURE 6.9

Now, let's look at an example of how the density of hatching lines can gradually increase to shade a spherical surface (Figure 6.10).

FIGURE 6.10

Crosshatching

Crosshatching is similar to hatching. It works the same way. The only difference is that the hatching lines intersect to form the shading. Again, the density of crosshatching determines the darkness of the shade. Figure 6.11 depicts an example of crosshatching.

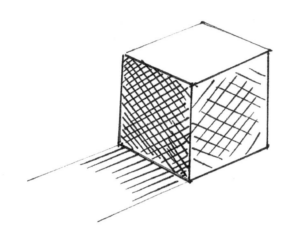

FIGURE 6.11

Contour Shading

The lines used to create hatching can also follow the contour of the underlying form. Notice how curved hatching lines follow the outline of the sphere in Figure 6.12.

Now, let's have some fun. I included a more complex form, as you'll see in Figure 6.13. Notice how the hatching lines follow the contour of the ribbon.

FIGURE 6.12

Scribbled Shading

One last technique is to use basic scribbles. This works nicely if you're working with graphite and pencils. Softer pencils can be used to create darker scribbles. Just as with the aforementioned techniques, the higher the density of scribbles, the darker the shadow will appear. Figure 6.14 depicts how scribbles can be used to add shading to a ribbon form.

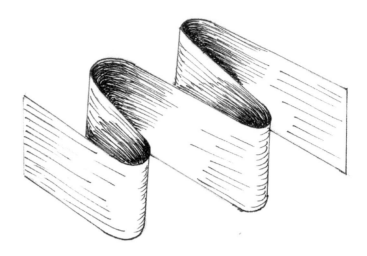

FIGURE 6.13

FIGURE 6.14

You can even use your finger to smudge or blend the shading for a smoother gradient. Personally, I'm a fan of texture, so I left behind visible pencil strokes in my shading. Just for good measure, I even threw in some shading around the object to describe the surface it's resting on.

USING ELEVATION

In the UX world, elevation is a concept used to improve the usability of a UI. It can be used to describe an element's hierarchical importance. This powerful concept is even highlighted in popular design systems like Google's

Material Design. We can add elevation to any element by providing a sense of light and shading. If you think about it, most elements on a screen are layered on top of each other as depicted by the cross section concept drawing in Figure 6.15. Elevation can be considered an affordance within a UI that improves the overall usability. It can shed light on areas that have scrolling content. Let's take a look at how it can be applied to a few basic UI elements.

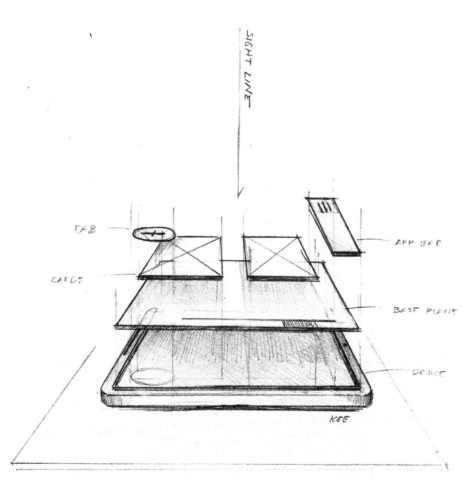

FIGURE 6.15

Modals and Dialogs

Modals and dialogs are common elements found in most desktop user interfaces. These elements are panels that pop up when you click or tap an option on the screen. They usually contain additional information and contextual actions. Modals and dialogs usually appear to be elevated off of the rest of the screen. To draw one of these elements, let's start by drawing a box inside of a box as illustrated in Figure 6.16.

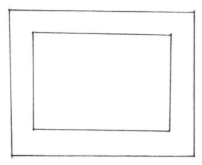

FIGURE 6.16

Next, let's add shading along the left and bottom outer edges of the inner box as drawn in Figure 6.17. Feel free to use the shading method of your choice. The inner panel should now appear elevated.

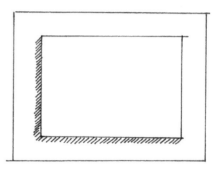

FIGURE 6.17

In this example I used hatching to create the drop shadow. Assuming the light source is located to the upper right of the image in Figure 6.17, the shadow would be cast to the lower-left of the inner box. I was mindful of the direction of the hatching lines I used to create my shading. This accentuates the direction of the cast shadow and makes it more believable to the viewer.

How about we bring this panel to life and make it look like a dialog? To do this, let's add a title at the top of the inner box and some buttons in the lower-right corner of the inner box, as depicted in Figure 6.18. I'm going to fill in the right button to suggest that it's a primary action.

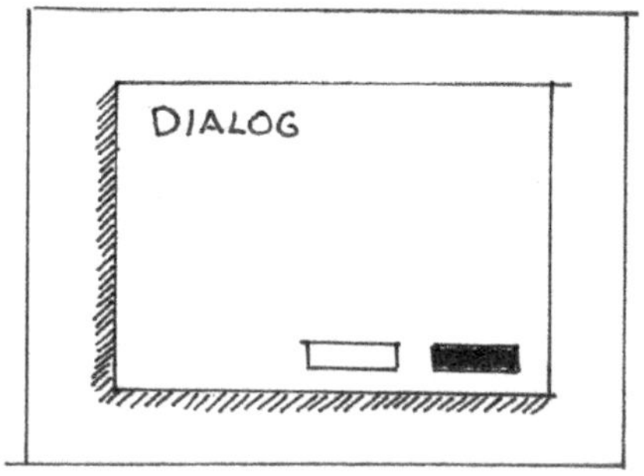

FIGURE 6.18

Some modals and dialogs use shading to draw more attention to themselves. In Figure 6.19, I'm using hatching to fill in the space between the inner and outer boxes.

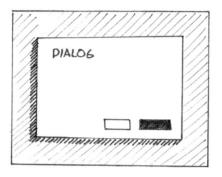

FIGURE 6.19

In this case, I leveraged the range of tools mentioned in Chapter 3. I started with a heavy weight 0.5 mm Pigma Micron pen. I used the same pen to create the initial drop shadow. I used a pen with a thinner 0.35 mm point to add the additional shadow hatching texture that appears between the inner dialog box and the outer screen border. This difference in line weight adds an extra sense of polish to the drawing. It also helps the viewer understand the difference between the shadow and the shades used in this drawing.

Fixed Position Elements

Accent lines can be used to represent stationary or "sticky" elements in the UI. By running a parallel accent line beneath the header of an app bar, we can imply that its position is fixed, as depicted in Figure 6.20.

FIGURE 6.20

We can also add a scroll bar drawing (Chapter 4, "Building from Rectangles") and a few list items as illustrated in Figure 6.21. When we do this, the drawing infers the app bar is always visible and the list content scrolls beneath it.

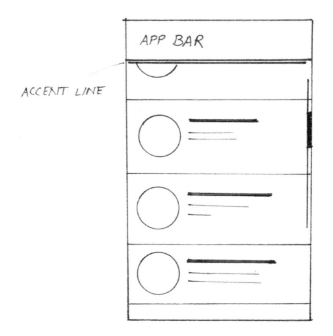

FIGURE 6.21

Alternatively, instead of using an accent line beneath the app bar, we can use our favorite shading technique to create a drop shadow, as depicted in Figure 6.22.

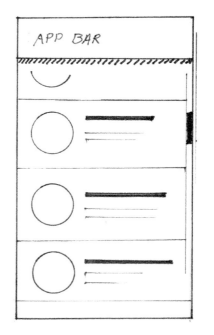

FIGURE 6.22

Cards

Remember the card stack example from Chapter 4? It's depicted in Figure 6.23. Let's add some additional touches to show that the cards are elevated.

FIGURE 6.23

We can add some hatching coming off of the left and bottom sides of the cards in the stack to give it a sense of depth, as drawn in Figure 6.24.

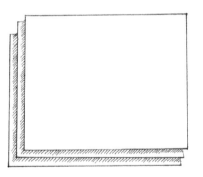

FIGURE 6.24

Interaction Hands and Cursors

We can introduce the concept of elevation when drawing cursor hands to represent mouse interactions (Figure 6.25).

After all, the mouse cursor floats above the UI, so we should represent it that way. We can apply a drop shadow using the hatching technique as depicted in Figure 6.26.

We can also use the same technique when suggesting gestural interactions within our digital product drawings. We can see an illustrated example of this applied to a mobile app layout as drawn in Figure 6.27.

FIGURE 6.25

FIGURE 6.26

In this case, the purpose of the sketch was to propose a novel scrolling interaction, so I exaggerated the shadows used on our gestural interaction. The arrow shows the direction of the gesture that causes the scrolling and the popping out of the video player window.

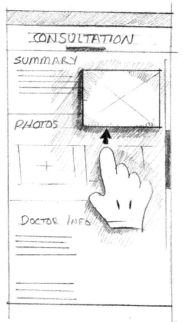

FIGURE 6.27

Other UI Elements

Other UI elements that are typically elevated include action buttons, alerts, onboarding information, and status indicators. Using the aforementioned techniques, we can give these elements a sense of elevation as highlighted in Figure 6.28.

These techniques can be used on any UI element you want to appear elevated or on its own vertical plane. Go ahead, give it a try!

USING TEXTURE

Believe it or not, there are a few cases in which texture can be used to help your colleagues understand your UX drawings. For example, textures can be applied to interactive elements like buttons and actions, giving them a tactile look and feel in your drawing. Figure 6.29 depicts a UI with textured avatar images that double as selection controls. To show that the icons are interactive, I used a texture.

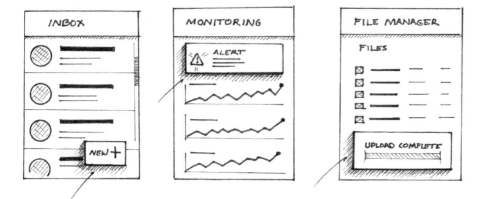

FIGURE 6.28

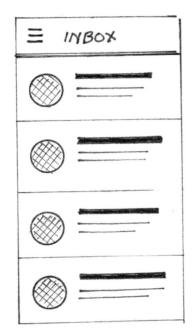

FIGURE 6.29

Adding these textures can help others further understand which elements in the proposed product drawing are touchable or interactive.

Textures can be used for conveying semantic meaning. If you're drawing a product with charts, graphs, and visualizations, textures can help your colleagues understand how they might visualize the different categories of data within your product. This can be especially useful when drawing charts that will show categories of information, such as stacked bar charts, stacked area charts, pie charts, and donut charts; Figure 6.30 shows a stacked bar chart.

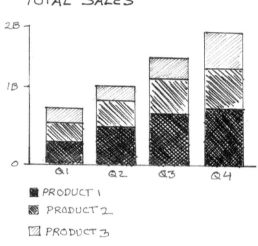

FIGURE 6.30

Textures can be used to represent physical materials. Let's draw another box. By placing a few diagonal lines near the top-left and lower-right corners of the box, as you'll see in Figure 6.31, we can imply that the rectangle is made of glass or some sort of glossy material. The lines can vary in length for added effect. This is a highly stylized solution that works in a pinch.

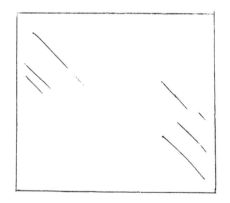

FIGURE 6.31

There are plenty of other ways to include texture in your drawings. These are just a few useful suggestions to get you started. After more practice and experience, you'll be able to come up with plenty of other ways to use textures to convey a new idea.

CAPTURING MOTION

This is one of the most fun concepts to capture. In a digital product drawing, we can describe transitional states between screens. Motion allows us to suggest how animated transitions may work, look, and feel. Let's try representing the concept of motion in a drawing. We'll start by drawing a railroad boxcar. To do this, we will draw a rectangle. Then, just for fun, we'll add a few small lines and circles representing wheels, as depicted in Figure 6.32.

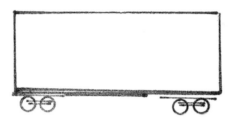

FIGURE 6.32

Now, let's add motion lines behind the boxcar to imply its forward motion. To do this properly, it's important to start the lines near the object, then draw away from it as illustrated in Figure 6.33. The direction of the lines implies motion.

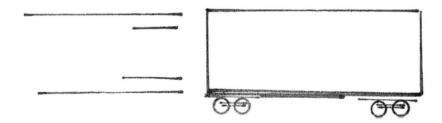

FIGURE 6.33

In addition to adding motion lines, you can imply motion by distorting the shape itself. In the example in Figure 6.34, I distorted my box, offsetting the top horizontal line of the box to imply forward motion and speed.

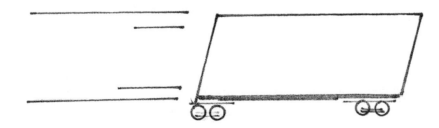

FIGURE 6.34

Figure 6.34 is an example of a motion line in a UX drawing. Some UIs feature spinning panels. Figure 6.35 highlights an example of the transition from one panel to another using a spin transition, and we can see that curved motion lines were added to further describe the transition.

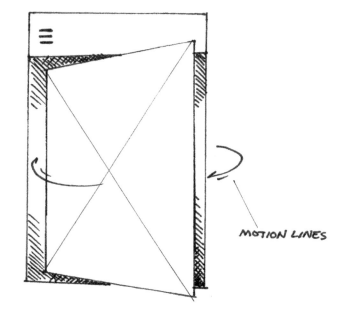

FIGURE 6.35

CONVEYING LUMINANCE

Let's take a look at how we can convey a sense of brightness within a product drawing. We can do this by applying a few minimal lines. In addition to providing a light source, the concept of luminance can help us understand the importance of an element in our proposed digital product. For example, luminance may be applied to an icon that may light up in order to grab someone's attention when there is an active alert. It can even be applied to physical products that have LEDs that light up in order to provide visual feedback.

Let's jump in. If we draw accent lines radiating off of a shape such as the circle in Figure 6.36, it implies that the circle is illuminated.

Longer lines placed farther away from the light source infer a higher level of brightness (Figure 6.37). This is a great way to communicate the concept of light without adding any shading to your drawing.

We can do the same with an alert icon, as depicted in Figure 6.38.

FIGURE 6.36

FIGURE 6.37

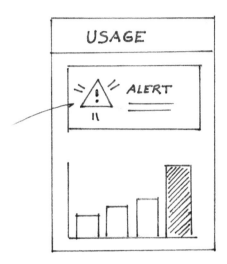

FIGURE 6.38

COMMUNICATING SOUND

We can use similar techniques to communicate sound by borrowing from the methods used to communicate the idea of luminance. When applied to alert notifications, we can use the same drawing we used for luminance to describe that the notification plays sound when it is displayed (Figure 6.39).

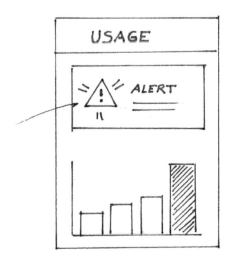

FIGURE 6.39

We can use different line styles to symbolize audio feedback as well. Take a look at an alternative method displayed in Figure 6.40.

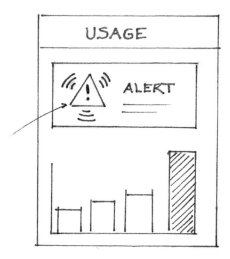

FIGURE 6.40

These are just a few ways to represent concepts in your drawings. Shading is the technique used to bring most of these concepts to life. Using accent lines to represent luminance, motion, and sound can help you provide additional details in your drawing.

Just as artists use these same techniques to enable people to engage with their artwork, we can use them to enable our colleagues to connect with our ideas on a much deeper level.

I had the chance to connect with a longtime friend and colleague, Borbay, *Time Out's* most creative New Yorker of 2009, successful painter, NFT artist, and gallery owner. He leverages many of these concepts in his own paintings. According to Borbay, when you correctly deliver light, you deliver something more than a painting. You capture emotion, and these visuals become living breathing experiences for the viewer. Borbay's painting in Figure 6.41 provides a great example of this. In product drawing, this can be helpful when using drawings to sell your next great idea.

Borbay also uses texture to create a sense of depth and light in his works, which also invoke certain feelings in the viewer. Through the use of creative license and exaggerating concepts like light and texture, Borbay explains that you can create a painting of a field that will make the viewer cry, while depicting a lighting storm in a way that brings joy to the viewer. All of this takes practice, of course, but it's a skill that you can build as you become more comfortable over time with drawing in your day-to-day work.

FIGURE 6.41
Source: *Radio City Music Hall,* Borbay, 2020

CONVERSATION WITH JASON BORBAY

Jason Borbay is an artist, author, and entrepreneur. In the following interview, he shares his ideas about techniques he uses in his paintings, including lighting and texturing, and how these can be applied in product and UX drawings.

How might some of the techniques used in your paintings be leveraged in product and UX drawings to help people understand the essence of an idea?

My work is process-driven. If you go to borbay.com and click on a painting, you will discover a step-by-step visual overview of its creation. The image is broken down into essential shapes and laid out with a warm under-painting. Next, each element is carefully drawn, and the shadows are blocked out. From there, every element is developed in concert with the entire canvas to deliver a cohesive vision. This applies to anything. If you want to create a website, you begin with a pencil sketch of the idea, followed by a screen layout, which is then blue-boxed into a functional model to explore the flow. Concurrently, the look and feel is developed and eventually applied to the functional model to deliver the final experience. By dissecting something complex into its most basic elements, your vision will grow. And, as we all know, it's far more cost effective to modify a UX design than it is to change a fully designed product after the fact.

Lighting seems to be a dominant element in all of your artwork. Can you tell me how light plays a role in describing the forms depicted in your compositions? Speak to if/how you use lighting as a method for storytelling or invoking a specific feeling in the viewers?

Without light there is darkness. Black is the absence of light, but it can be experienced in light. Light is complex. When a child draws a face, they put the eyes at the top of the head, draw lips and hair are also disconnected. It doesn't feel right. When you study light, whether you are creating a face or a neon sign, it's all about shapes. The more severe the light, the more dramatic the shapes. When you correctly deliver light, you create something more than a painting—you capture emotion. Successful visuals across all disciplines make you feel. They emote. They are living, breathing experiences for the viewer, even when they are static

Can you tell me more about how you might exaggerate elements in your paintings for effect? Why do you do this?

We have a little thing called the "creative license," and I'm going to push the boundaries until it is revoked. This could include omitting elements of the composition while exaggerating others. This is where fine art can transcend photography and digital work. A painting of a field can make someone cry, a terrible lightning storm can bring

joy; It's all about the execution, and the finest work is the result of painstaking analysis and scores of hours toiling to master your craft.

How do texture and brush strokes play a role in your painting? I noticed some of your paintings, like the *Biltmore Putting Green at Twilight* (see the figure), are rich in texture, while others, like the Radio City painting are not.

There is an Italian term, *impasto*, that essentially means creating depth through texture. In my gestural works, the mood changes dramatically, as a simple brush stroke can introduce an element of depth, light, and shadow within the picture plane. In other works, I'm intentionally deliberate with my brush strokes, allowing the light, space, and composition to breathe without variation on the surface. It's akin to being a pitcher in baseball... if you have a pitcher who throws some serious heat, but the other team's big slugger can't hit a curveball, it's on you to curate the correct pitches that will result in an out.

Source: Biltmore putting green at twilight, Borbay, 2021

Can you tell me about how your painting style has developed over time? How have painting and drawing techniques and style matured and evolved throughout the years?

Sometimes, I feel like I haven't evolved at all; that is, until I go back in time and re-read my painting recap posts. My process continues to evolve and become more sophisticated: the amoeba becomes a fish, which journeys out of the water as a lizard, begins to walk upright and, well, you know the rest. This is particularly evident in Borbay Studios & Gallery. when I look at a work from even 2020 next to what I've created since, the advancement is noticeable. That's the beauty of life; if you continue to learn you will grow—and excellence will find you. I can't wait to see what I'm capable of in 2030 and beyond.

Further thinking about how to illustrate these concepts can help you start a deeper conversation with your colleagues about how your product will look, work, and respond to its users. You can even suggest how one might feel while using your product.

Applying these concepts may feel intimidating at first, and yes, it will take some practice. You can develop these skills over time. It's important to remember that we can all draw, and as Borbay suggests, we probably had our artistic development unintentionally stunted by an early-age, throwaway comment, like, "That's not the best." Or, perhaps we experienced an overwhelming feeling of inadequacy compared to our peers' ability. If our artistic ability is frozen in time, we can unfreeze it by proceeding with an open mind and giving it another go.

CHAPTER SEVEN

THE SYSTEM

L et's pause for a moment and take stock of everything we've covered up until now. So far in this book, we took an in-depth look at a comprehensive set of reusable elements, or building blocks, that can be used in all of our digital product drawings. We also reviewed several ways to describe concepts like light, sound, texture, and motion.

You are now armed with the right toolkit for creating a full product drawing. Let's think of your visual library as a system as illustrated in Figure 7.1. Just like the components in a design system, they can be combined in different ways to develop, share, and collaborate on an infinite amount of ideas. That's the focus of this chapter.

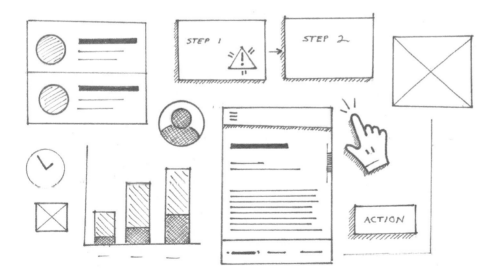

FIGURE 7.1

PUTTING IT TOGETHER

Not sold on this? Let's create a fairly detailed UX drawing. Moving forward, we are going to leverage our drawing system to create multiple drawings to convey an idea. Now, most UX drawings represent some sort of user journey, task, or flow. We will discuss this more in the next chapter. For this example, let's pretend we're designing a new email app for mobile devices.

Before we jump in, let's define the task we're going to illustrate. In this case, we'll show how someone can locate, read, and reply to an email in a hypothetical new email experience. To do this, let's first brainstorm the process for responding to an email. Then we will map it in a process diagram. Remember, if you can draw boxes and arrows, you can draw a process diagram.

Think about the last time you checked your email. Once you opened your email app, I'm going to guess that you looked at your inbox first and scanned all the unread messages. This will be the first step in our diagram, as illustrated in Figure 7.2.

FIGURE 7.2

Next, I'm going to guess that you found a message that captured your attention. Maybe it was something urgent; you tapped on it and read it. That will be the next step illustrated in our diagram, as shown in Figure 7.3.

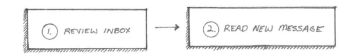

FIGURE 7.3

Finally, I'm going to go ahead and guess you replied to the message. That will be our third and final step in the process diagram. Let's number the steps in our diagram as illustrated in Figure 7.4. If you need a refresher on process diagrams, please refer back to Chapter 2, "Reframing Our Thinking."

FIGURE 7.4

Now, let's draw some screens that correspond with each step in our process diagram. First, to draw the inbox screen, we'll use an app bar, list view, and floating button. Since the app bar and button appear to float above the rest of the scrolling content, we'll draw them first, as you will see in Figure 7.5.

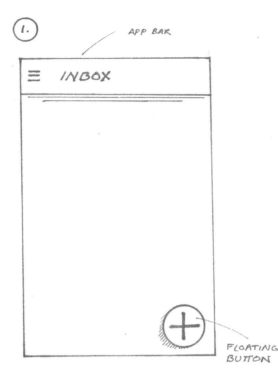

FIGURE 7.5

In doing this, these objects will appear in front of the other elements. I even added some accent lines beneath the app bar and some hatching to the lower left of the floating button to show that they're elevated.

Next, we'll add some list items and a scroll bar, as drawn in Figure 7.6. Since the list scrolls behind the floating button, none of the elements within the list item should be drawn on top of the floating button. To make life easier, consider creating the drawing with a pencil so you can erase any mistakes. You can always go over your pencil lines with ink later on.

Since the list of messages in the inbox screen scrolls, we'll add our symbol for a scroll bar, and we'll use some hatching to show that the app bar remains in a fixed position and the content scrolls beneath it, as highlighted in Figure 7.6.

Finally, we can add a cursor hand to show which list item was tapped to get to the next screen, as you will see in Figure 7.7.

I chose to add it over the second list item. Don't forget, we can use hatching to apply a drop shadow coming off the lower-left side of the cursor hand. This implies that the cursor hand is not part of the actual screen layout.

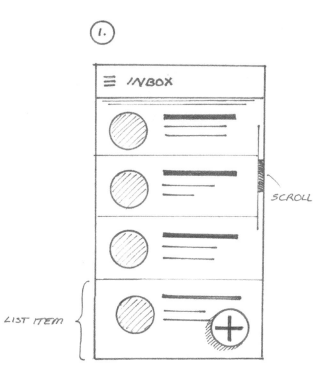

FIGURE 7.6

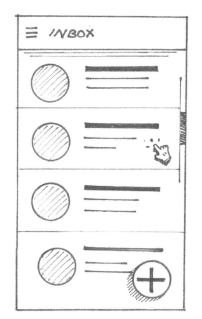

FIGURE 7.7

Now, let's move to step 2 and represent the next screen in the flow. To represent the actual message, we'll do a few things. First, we'll draw a new screen. Instead of using a standard menu icon, or hamburger, in the app bar, we'll draw a backward arrow. Also, be sure to add a label here as you see in Figure 7.8. That way we can show that we're now on a new screen and that there's a way for users to get back to the previous screen.

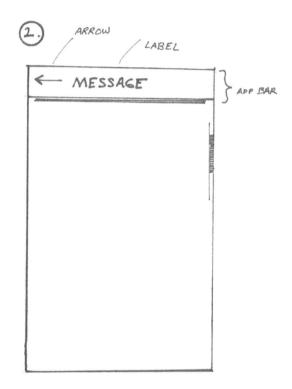

FIGURE 7.8

To start filling in content, let's draw a message header area. This will appear just beneath the app bar and above the actual message. This would include the avatar image of the message's sender, the subject line, time stamps, and so on. We'll use the same elements from our list item on the previous screen to represent this. The message info area is labeled in Figure 7.9.

Next, let's fill in some message content. To do this, we'll draw a series of lines to represent the message's content. All lines should be left aligned but may vary in length, as you see labeled in Figure 7.9.

Finally, we'll add some buttons beneath the text block to suggest actions that can be taken. Be sure to draw a cursor hand pointing to the reply button. You may even consider using shading and writing out the word *reply* within the button, as drawn in Figure 7.10.

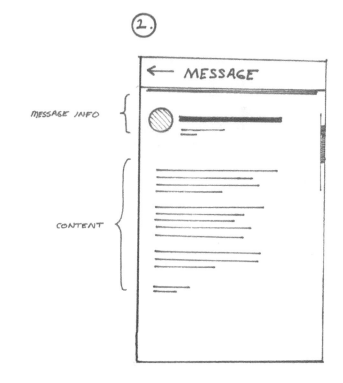

FIGURE 7.9

FIGURE 7.10

Finally, let's draw the third and last step. To do this, we'll draw a new screen, and we'll arrange a few symbols representing form controls. Let's start by drawing another app bar. We'll use an arrow and add a *Reply* label as highlighted in Figure 7.11.

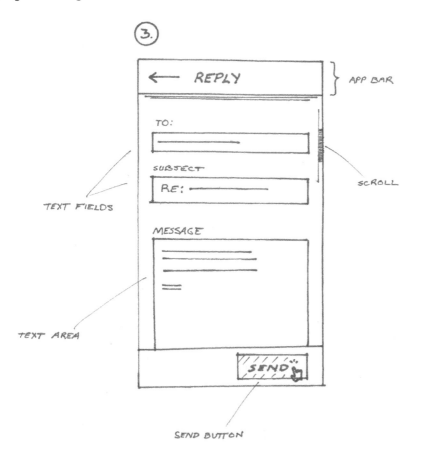

FIGURE 7.11

Next, we'll add some of the form controls covered previously in Chapter 4, "Building from Rectangles." We'll add two text fields that represent the recipient's line and subject line, as pictured in Figure 7.11. Next, we'll add a text area. This represents the area where the reply will be crafted. Instead of using lines to represent form labels, I chose to write them out. This further describes the purpose of each field to the viewer.

Finally, as pictured in Figure 7.11, we'll add a send button beneath the text area. I even added a cursor hand pointing to the Send button so that we know how the illustrated task is completed.

Now, let's put it all together. If you didn't already, let's arrange the process diagram and corresponding screen designs into an organized flow as depicted in Figure 7.12.

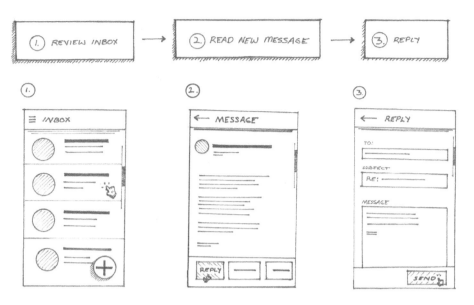

FIGURE 7.12

If you used separate papers to create your process diagrams and screen drawings, go ahead and cut them out. You can start with the process diagram and then paste each screen cutout beneath the corresponding step. Be sure to number the screens so they correspond with the steps in the process diagram as depicted in Figure 7.12. Instead of cutting and pasting, you can also redraw the diagram and screens arranged on the same paper. If you have a dedicated workspace or studio with a bare wall, you can hang all of your drawings up on the wall and take a photo.

That's it! We just created our first flow of screens. This is a rich UX drawing that describes the steps taken to reply to an urgent message within our pretend email app design. In this drawing, we get a sense of the overarching process as well as how each screen looks and behaves. We even highlighted key interaction points that moved us forward in the illustrated process. By showing the elevation of elements like the app bar on certain screens, we also provide additional details on how each screen behaves.

CREATING SOMETHING NEW

As you can see, the system of concepts and elements in your visual library is very versatile. It especially works well when drawing screens and UX elements that were popular at the time in which this book was written. As time goes on, and technology evolves, you're going to encounter situations where you may have to create a new symbol, element, or icon on your own.

To do this, think about the basic shapes you can combine to draw new elements. Nearly everything you draw can be distilled down to a few basic shapes and marks. Think about how you can leverage the basic concepts covered in this book.

Recently, I was thinking of ways to visualize the effects of precipitation on a network of high altitude flight vehicles and satellites. I knew I'd want to create some sort of 3D weather visualization that highlighted the vehicles and their locations and ability to communicate with each other. I also knew I wanted to overlay weather information on the same visualization. This would include wind and precipitation information; I wasn't sure how I wanted to do it.

I turned to drawing to help me think through a few ideas. While brainstorming methods for visualizing weather systems and satellite networks, I turned to nature to provide inspiration for my end solution.

The murmuration of starlings in Figure 7.13 gave me the idea to represent precipitation and cloud moisture using a particle system. As far as I could think, this seemed like a promising start, but I needed to see it on paper. Now, looking at the image in Figure 7.13, you might recognize that the starlings look like dots. Some areas of the murmuration have higher concentrations of birds than others. This seemed to translate well into a weather visualization, where particles could be used to represent a storm system. The denser the particles, the higher the cloud moisture, precipitation rate, and so on. This could also work well in 3D.

FIGURE 7.13

Now for the drawing part, let's imagine each starling as a point in a drawing, as highlighted in Figure 7.14. Does this remind you of a shading technique we discussed in the previous chapter?

FIGURE 7.14

For my actual product drawing, which is featured in Figure 7.15, you can now see how I used pointillism to demonstrate my idea. The points represent the particle system, and you can see how it fits into the visualization of my satellite network. In this drawing, the storm is impacting a satellite's ability to communicate with a ground station.

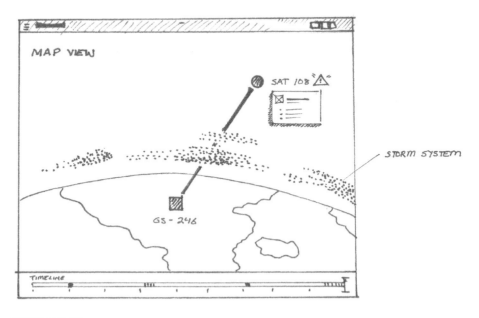

FIGURE 7.15

This is a fine example of a time when I was working with a team on a completely new product with cutting-edge technology. One of my colleagues even referred to it as science fiction. When brainstorming solutions during this project, I turned to drawing to help me develop my ideas. I leveraged the basic shapes and marks covered earlier in this book to represent a new idea. While I didn't have a preset icon or symbol in mind for representing weather in a visualization, I turned to the basic marks I used to draw common shapes, and I applied them in a new way.

As time goes on, and you become more comfortable with drawing, think about how you can leverage marks, concepts, and the basic shapes and elements previously covered to create something completely new. Of course, if it works for you, this new drawing might become a core part of your library moving forward. In the next chapters, we're going to look at even more ways to apply your visual library in a systematic way to tell compelling stories.

CHAPTER EIGHT

USING FLOWS TO TELL STORIES

Now that we covered the "how to draw" content, let's have some fun. We now have a working visual library of elements, and we reviewed ways to combine them and create an array of screens and detailed UX drawings. Let's take a look at how we can use this knowledge to start telling stories.

In the last chapter, we created a basic flow. We started with a process diagram and then drew screens based on each step in the illustrated process. Most digital experiences are designed based on the key needs of the people using our proposed product, website, or experience. The solutions we create should help these people accomplish their high-priority goals and tasks.

Our designs should be built around these goals and tasks. Because of this, we usually present our designs as a flow of screens, or steps, in a process that represent our proposed method for completing a task or accomplishing a goal in our proposed product. For example, let's revisit our inbox app flow from the last chapter (Figure 8.1). This design was optimized for someone who wanted to complete the task of finding an important email and replying to it.

To bring this flow to life, you first need to understand the syntax of a great screen flow, and then we'll review some additional elements that increased the impact of this drawing.

STARTING WITH THE SYNTAX

Just as there are different written languages, such as English, Spanish, French, and German, there are different visual languages. This book refers to the visual language of digital products and UX design. Let's think about the building blocks of our visual library. We can consider these items the "words" of our visual language. If we refer back to our inbox flow, shown in Figure 8.2, the interface elements, such as the email list, the message, and form controls, are the nouns. Concepts like light, motion, elevation, and texture describe these nouns. These are the adjectives of our visual language. Finally, the actions we take to move us forward in the flow, like tapping buttons, gestural interactions, scrolling, and typing our reply, are the verbs in our visual language.

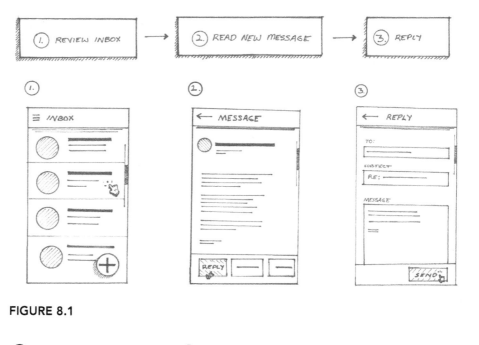

FIGURE 8.1

FIGURE 8.2

A good flow starts with syntax. Just as the right syntax of nouns, verbs, and adjectives enables us to craft a coherent sentence, the right syntax of visual elements enables us to craft a coherent flow that describes the completion of a task or goal in our digital product. If we were to omit a word from a sentence, the sentence might lose its meaning. The same is true for our flows. If we omit a step from our flow, it will also lose some of its meaning. Let's take a look.

Using our inbox example, if we were to omit step 2 from the original inbox example in Figure 8.2, the flow becomes much more difficult to understand, as you can see in Figure 8.3. When looking at this, you might wonder how we got from the inbox screen on the left directly to the reply screen on the right. There's no visible option to directly reply to a message available on the inbox screen drawing.

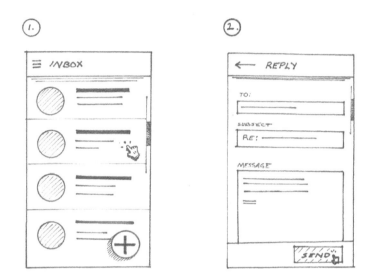

FIGURE 8.3

It's not only a matter of missing screens, there are key elements in each screen that help us understand the syntax of this flow. For example, if we were to remove the app bars atop each of the drawings as shown in Figure 8.4, we lose our sense of orientation within the flow. Wayfinding in this flow is much more difficult.

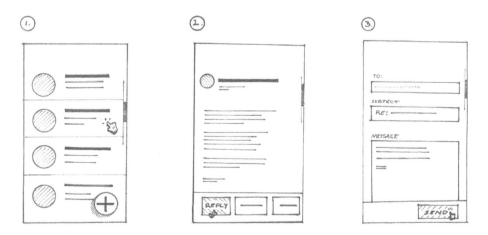

FIGURE 8.4

Remember, when you're sharing a new idea, your teammates cannot read your mind. They're seeing a representation of your idea for the very first time. It's important to make sure all the necessary elements are in each screen and each step is represented.

In the tech industry, the lingo we use to describe our work is constantly evolving. Not everyone will be up to speed on that lingo. Your drawings can further define the lingo you're using. At the time in which this book was written, the metaverse and Web3 were all the rage. Not everyone knew what that referred to at first. Drawing can be used to better articulate ideas created for evolving tech platforms and new surfaces and spaces. To do this right, the bottom line is this: our teammates need to see all the screens and understand all the steps taken to complete the goal or task at hand in our proposed product, even if some of the steps seem redundant.

SHOWING INTERACTIONS

Interactions are the glue that holds our flows and storyboards together. These are the aforementioned verbs in our visual language. They are a crucial part of any UX drawing because they are a representation of how people will interact with our products. They also show how someone will move forward to the next step in order to accomplish their goal. Helping your teammates understand how someone will arrive on a screen and how they will get to the next screen will help them better understand your ideas.

To represent interactions, we will use drawings of different cursor types and gestures as depicted in Figure 8.5 to represent different types of interaction in our flows. Drawing these individual items was covered in more detail in Chapter 5, "Building from Circles, Triangles, and More."

FIGURE 8.5

In our inbox example, you'll notice we showed a small touch interaction on each screen. We can assume that this is the interaction that moves us to the next step. In Figure 8.6, I enlarged the interactions to place more focus on them.

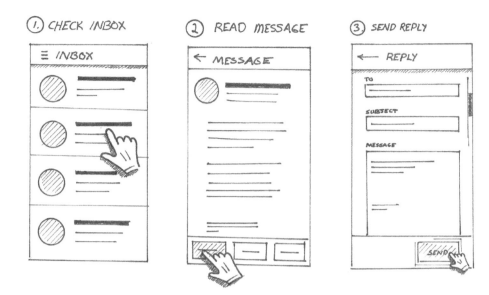

FIGURE 8.6

Another way we can place focus on the sequence is to connect each screen by drawing arrows directly from the interaction to the next screen, as depicted in Figure 8.7. It's up to you to determine how much focus is appropriate to place on the interactions depicted in your flow. This does take some focus off of some of the interface details in each screen, but it's effective in showing the ease of interaction within the flow.

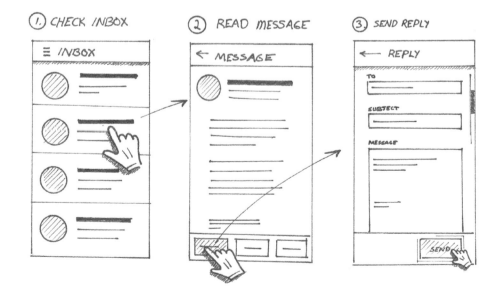

FIGURE 8.7

Let's imagine we're creating a flow that represents the key screens of a new photos app. The flow we will see in Figure 8.8 demonstrates how someone would find the perfect photo from last month's trip to share with family and friends. Since the app will run on a mobile device, the design will rely on gestures like swiping and scrolling to find the photo. Notice how they are represented in Figure 8.8.

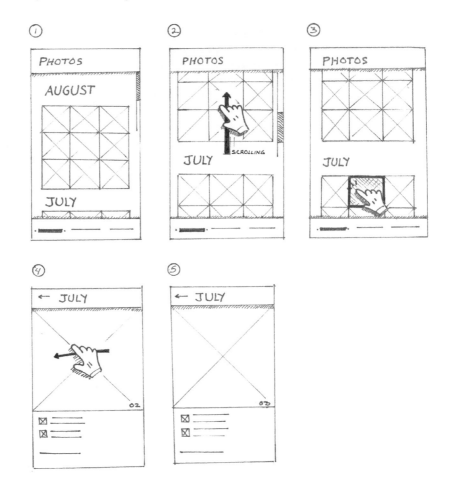

FIGURE 8.8

JUST ENOUGH INFORMATION

If you look at steps 4 and 5 in Figure 8.8, you'll notice they look very similar. It's difficult to discern how the steps differ from each other. The gesture depicted in step 4 and the numbers 02 and 03 in the bottom-right corner of the images in steps 4 and 5 are our only indications that something has changed. Sometimes, in a case like this, we need to make it more obvious that something has changed as a result of the swipe interaction between steps 4 and 5. In this particular flow, the user can swipe to access the next image. To make this more obvious, I'm going to use some basic marks and shading to suggest the content in each of the photos as depicted in Figure 8.9.

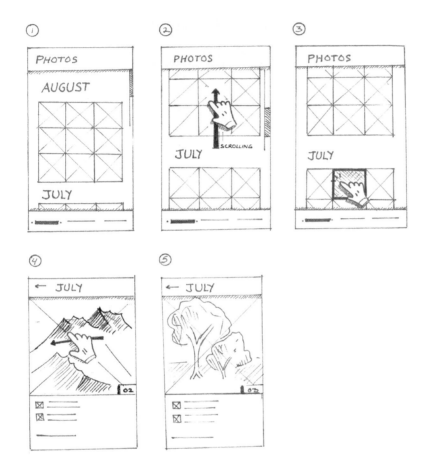

FIGURE 8.9

The key is that the two images look drastically different from one another. That way, people looking at this image can understand that the swipe gesture led us to an entirely new image. For the first image in step 4, let's suggest some mountains. In the image in step 5, let's suggest some trees. You can rough in different shapes or whatever you wish to suggest the change in images.

DEPICTING TRANSITIONS

In some cases, animation is used to help strengthen people's mental model of an interface, and if done well, it can be used to help teach people how it works. Because of this, there are times when we should consider representing animation in our drawings, especially when it's a crucial part of our proposed design. We can use arrows and motion lines (Figure 8.10) to demonstrate how animated transitions might work.

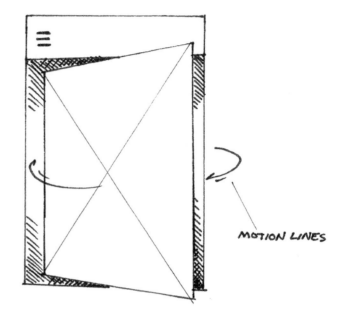

FIGURE 8.10

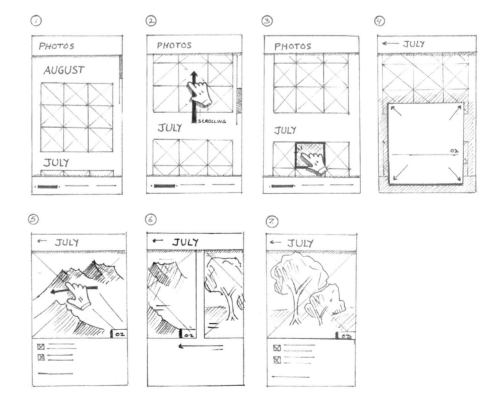

FIGURE 8.11

Now, let's revisit our photos app flow. While the gestures do a fine job connecting the screens in our flow, there's still some missing information that will better describe the specifics of this flow. Let's add a few key transitional screens into our flow as you see in Figure 8.11. This will enable us to further describe the relationship between the interactions, the subsequent animations, and the transitions from the photo grid to individual photos.

In this example, we added two transitional screens. The first is depicted in step 4 of Figure 8.11. It shows the photo that was tapped in step 3. The photo morphs into a card. It's moving forward and taking over the screen. This helps us better understand how we transitioned from step 3 to step 5. In this transition frame, additional details of the photo card are coming into view. The arrows show the direction in which the photo card grows.

In Step 6, we see another transition screen. This time, we are seeing a depiction of the photos animating as a result of the swipe interaction in the previous step. This highlights how someone might swipe forward to navigate to the next photo in the card view. I also threw in the impression of the mountains and the trees to make the transition more believable. This also helps us understand that there's a difference between steps 5 and 7.

LABELS AND ANNOTATIONS

Since our visual library mostly consists of shapes and icons that carry symbolic meaning, we often need to add text and notes to further describe our ideas.

First and foremost, we can use labels in lieu of lines to represent screen titles and sections of content. Let's revisit our telemedicine app example. I isolated a key part of this drawing in Figure 8.12. Notice how I used handwritten labels to further describe the content sections like the video feed, summary, photos, and other details. These labels appear right in the drawing. I also used labels to show an outline of the content that will appear in this screen. This provides more detail on the hierarchy of information that would appear on this screen. This reference appears to the right of the drawing in Figure 8.12.

In addition to labels, annotations can be used to further highlight the thought process behind our drawings, the organization of our layouts, and their connection to real-world constraints and scenarios.

Figure 8.13, another isolated view of the full app drawing, points to the additional notes and doodles that begin to describe how the layout may work in landscape mode. These notes appear to the right of the consultation screen layout drawing. While the full landscape mode wasn't yet designed, these notes were used as a conversation starter to help my teammates and project stakeholders begin to brainstorm how a landscape view might work.

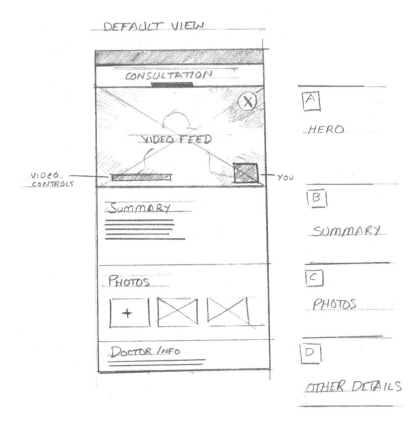

FIGURE 8.12

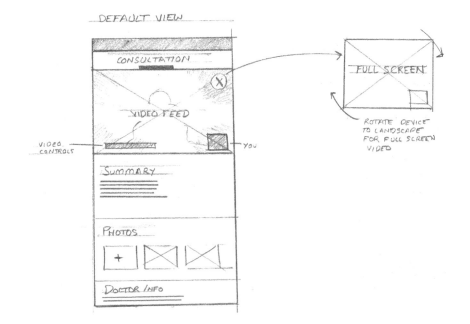

FIGURE 8.13

Let's go back to the full drawing as you will see it (Figure 8.14). Annotations help us understand that we're looking at two different versions of the same screen. The first drawing on the left is the default state of the screen. The second is a scrolling view that demonstrates how the video player remains fixed throughout a consultation as the rest of the screen scrolls. The labels above each screen and a few other noted details highlighted in Figure 8.14 help us understand this.

When you have the luxury of presenting your own drawings to your team, your annotations may be somewhat minimal. If your drawings are going to

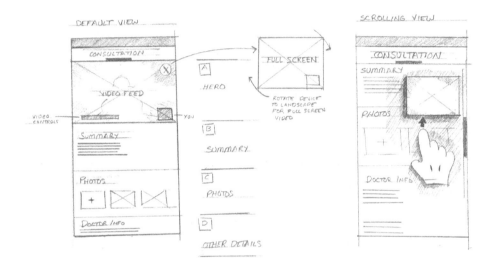

FIGURE 8.14

be part of a presentation that's left behind to be read later, your annotations might be much heavier because the people who will see it later may not have the context. In this case, the drawings are integrated into a slide deck that are part of a larger design presentation with plenty of complementary text.

While we're on the subject of text and annotations, I want to point out that handwriting matters. It's important that your notes and labels can be read by others, especially in your absence. While my handwriting is terrible at best, I always try to pull it together for my product drawings.

Here's something that helped me: I always admired the works of famous architects like Frank Lloyd Wright, who introduced several revolutionary new construction techniques. His ideas were clearly articulated through beautifully labeled drawings. Just as Wright was introducing a lot of new ideas in the architecture community, we are introducing a lot of new ideas in the tech industry.

At an early age I adopted a similar writing style. After all, most blueprints are labeled with all uppercase handwriting. The style invokes a serious and technical feel, something that I want to carry into my own work.

Label positioning and leveling is also important. It's okay to use a straightedge and a pencil to draw construction lines first, as suggested in Figure 8.15. Construction lines will provide a clean baseline for your handwritten label. We can use construction to align the height of the small and large capital letters in each label.

FIGURE 8.15

Finally, letter quality is important. We should always use clean lines to draw each letter form. It's okay if it takes longer to write each letter. Take your time! Clearly written labels will enable your teammates to do less work interpreting your drawing. Give it a try. You'll be surprised at how quickly you can elevate the quality of your existing drawings.

If you're still not feeling good about your handwriting or ability to add labels and annotations to your sketches, you might consider adding them digitally once your drawings are scanned and embedded in your design presentation.

BEING CONSCIOUS OF COMPOSITION

As you might imagine, our UX drawings can become quite detailed and complex. Illustrating a task, even with the most elegant of interface designs, may still require several drawings. It's important to think about where the sketches will live and what purpose they will serve. This will help you determine how to best arrange your flows.

For example, the composition we used earlier (Figure 8.16), where we show everything at once, including the workflow diagram and corresponding screens, works well if you have a dedicated UX space and you're going to hang up your drawings on a large wall. That method also works well if you're using a whiteboard.

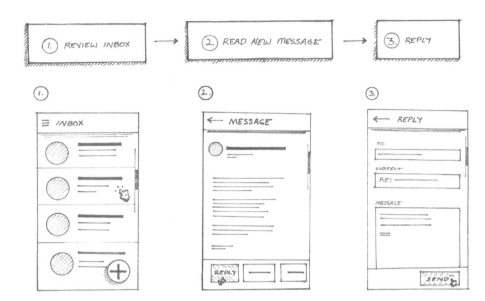

FIGURE 8.16

If you're going to be dropping your sketches into a digital slide deck, or if you're creating a multipage presentation doc, your flow might span several pages or slides. In this case, you might consider showing one screen per page as suggested in Figure 8.17. Notice how we're using the process diagram on each page for additional context and wayfinding purposes. The corresponding step is highlighted in the diagram at all times.

Minimaps can be a crucial wayfinding mechanism, especially in a long flow with many screens and steps. If your product's information architecture is more important to your team, you can show context and location by drawing on each page a mini–information architecture (IA) map instead of the process diagram. You can map the screen to its place in the IA for each process step illustrated, as suggested in Figure 8.18.

These are just a few examples of how you can create a flow. If the flow is going to break onto multiple pages, it's important to consider what element will provide the greater context on each page of the flow, whether it's a process diagram, IA map, or some other drawing. The possibilities here are endless, and I can't wait to see what you come up with as you start to include drawing in your product design process. I will provide more details on how you can combine different types of drawings with your flows to tell an engaging story in the next chapter.

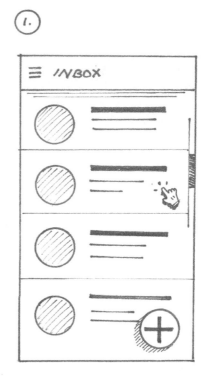

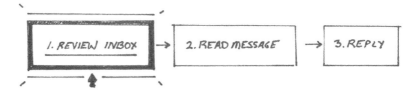

FIGURE 8.17

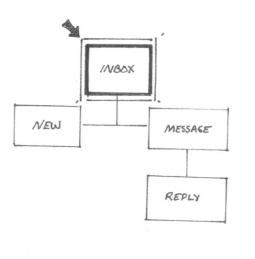

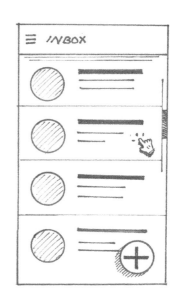

FIGURE 8.18

No matter what composition you use for your flow, there's a few tactical things you must consider in order to improve readability. Drawings can be quite complex, so it's important to provide a starting point in every flow. Think about the reading direction of your culture. Western cultures read from left to right and top to bottom. With this in mind, the first screen should appear at the left or top of your flow depending on its orientation, as you will see highlighted in Figure 8.19. I highly recommend numbering the steps to further establish the starting screen in the flow.

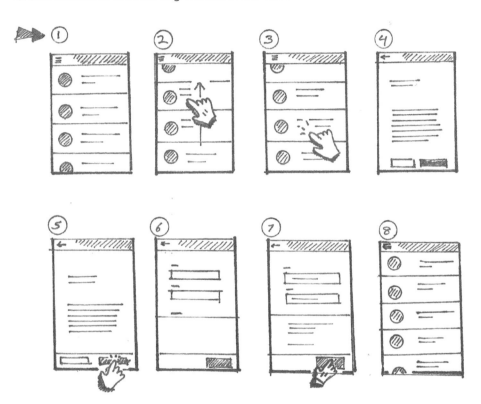

FIGURE 8.19

Highlighting the sequence and direction of the flow is also important. Numbering is a nice way to do this with linear flows. Some screen flows may include decision points and dependencies and highlight multiple outcomes. For these, I highly suggest using arrows to connect each of the screens, as highlighted in Figure 8.20.

Finally, readability can be improved through well-aligned drawings. Screens in a horizontal flow should be vertically aligned with each other. Screens on a vertical flow should be horizontally aligned with each other. Additionally, I suggest making sure some of the key elements in the screen are also aligned. That way your flow is optimized for readability. You'll want your teammates to focus on the content of the drawing rather than how it was drawn.

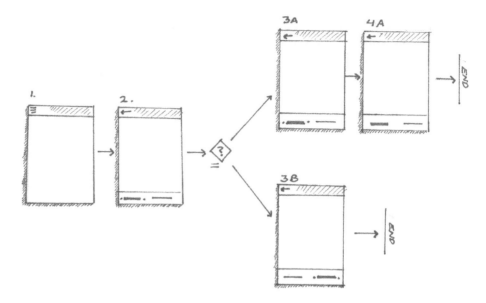

FIGURE 8.20

When I start a new drawing, especially for a design presentation, I use construction lines drawn with pencil to make sure my screens and their elements are properly aligned. Take a look at Figure 8.21. This example shows the construction lines I used to draw the flow depicted earlier in Figure 8.19. Once you apply ink to your drawing, these lines can be erased and no one will ever know they existed.

I can't stress enough the importance of this, especially if you're wondering how to draw with the elegance and polish of a seasoned UX designer. Clean alignments of screens and their key elements will enable people to focus more on the content of your flows and less on how they were drawn.

Using a flow is the best way to develop and share new designs for screen-based products. It helps you and your team focus on designing the best possible methods for your product's users to accomplish an important task or achieve their goals using your product.

Thinking about the syntax of your flow will help your teammates and stakeholders better understand your ideas. Annotations will help you further describe the steps and key details in your design. Considering where your drawings will live and how they will be consumed by your peers will enable you to make better decisions as to how to structure your flows and optimize their layouts for readability.

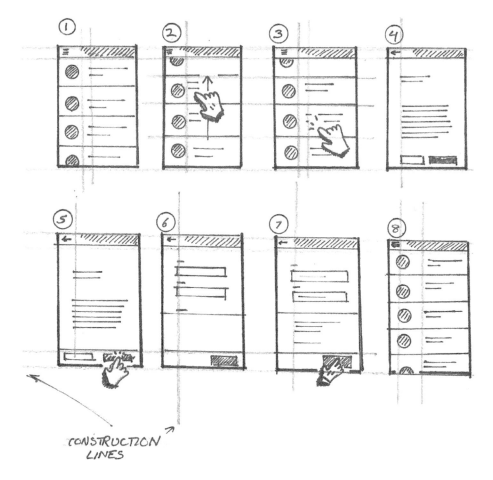

CONSTRUCTION
LINES

FIGURE 8.21

These considerations will enable you to elicit the right feedback from your team, and it will enable them to focus on what matters. Now that we covered the basics of a flow, let's talk about how to use what we already know in order to tell a rich story that will contribute to a better outcome.

CHAPTER NINE

TELLING ENGAGING STORIES

Now that we're assembling our drawings into flows, let's have some fun and take things a step further. Let's focus on the art of sharing drawings with colleagues and enabling them to connect with your ideas.

One of my favorite paintings is the *Great Wave Off Kanagawa*, as illustrated in Figure 9.1. Do you know what this painting is about? Take a guess. At first glance you might suspect that it is a depiction of a tidal wave, or a ship that's about to capsize. After all, these elements are prominently featured in the composition.

FIGURE 9.1
Source: *The Great Wave off Kanagawa*, by Katsushika Hokusai

It turns out that this is a depiction of Mount Fuji, which is pictured in the background. In fact, *The Great Wave Off Kanagawa* is one painting in a larger series, Thirty-Six Views of Mount Fuji. Figure 9.2, Figure 9.3, and Figure 9.4 highlight a few pieces from this series. You'll notice that each painting in

FIGURE 9.2
Source: Part of the series Thirty-Six Views of Mount Fuji, no. 02, by Katsushika Hokusai

FIGURE 9.3
Source: *Enoshima in Sagami Province*. Part of the series Thirty-Six Views of Mount Fuji, by Katsushika Hokusai

FIGURE 9.4
Source: *Honjo Tatekawa, the timberyard at Honjo,* by Katsushika Hokusai

the series features a unique composition that provides a view of Mount Fuji. The volcano is more prominently featured in some of the works and less in others. It typically appears as a background element.

Manuel Lima, who is well known for his work in data visualization and the author of the foreword to this book, also published a wonderful article comparing Mount Fuji to a data set. In the article, Manuel explained how there are infinite ways to view the data set, just as Hokusai, the artist, created different ways to view Mount Fuji in his series.

It turns out, just as Manuel thinks of a data set as Mount Fuji, we can think of our ideas as Mount Fuji. There are endless ways to view them. Our drawings may provide one or many views of an idea. We curate and arrange several of the elements in our visual library into a composition to create that unique point of view. This point of view is ultimately passed on to our colleagues that we're sharing the drawing with. What do we want them to see? What do we want them to take away from our ideas? How do we want them to feel about them? What is important for them to focus on? These are just a few of the considerations we will take into account when drawing our view of an idea.

The results of the compositional decisions set the purpose and meaning of the visual statement and carry strong implications for what the viewer receives. (Dondis 1973, 20) In order for our drawing to resonate with colleagues, it's important to give them a view of our idea that is realistic, engaging, and grounded in reality. Let's take a look at a few ways to do this.

This is going to be helpful when you're creating drawings to share with colleagues. It will help your teammates connect with your ideas on a deeper level, and it will enable them to provide more thoughtful feedback and give you the ability to build on your ideas more effectively, thus moving the design thinking process forward. After all, design happens best in a group. Let's jump in and explore techniques for making our drawings more effective through storytelling.

REAL-WORLD CONSTRAINTS

First and foremost, as we're creating our UX drawings, we always need to keep in mind real-world scenarios and constraints that will affect our decision-making throughout our product design process. Drawings that are not connected to reality will rarely lead to a successful outcome. Even when I'm facilitating a design workshop, I notice the drawings that lack consideration for real-world constraints are usually quickly discarded by the team. With that all being said, it's not difficult to connect your ideas to reality. Let's take a look at a few things to consider when grounding ideas in reality.

Start with Content—Everything Else Follows

Years ago, when I was just entering the professional world as a young designer, I cared a lot about visual design, maybe even too much for my own good. In fact, I was formally trained as a visual designer, and my degree is in fine arts. Shortly after graduating, I landed my first job at a small mom-and-pop shop advertising agency in a small Pennsylvania college town. I designed several microsites and online promotions for Scripps Networks, Lutron, and Yahoo!

During this time, I was encouraged to sketch my early ideas, just as we did in design school. I would review the copy deck created by the copywriter; then I'd start sketching different layout options and considerations for big ideas and visual design themes that would bring the copy to life. Sadly, in doing this, I wasn't as focused on the content itself as much as I was the overall design direction.

When I moved from concept sketches to creating computer-generated designs, I started working with actual content. During this time, I realized my early drawings were useless and got me nowhere in the process. They were just crude marks on a piece of paper and nothing more. They meant absolutely nothing because they were content-agnostic layouts. They didn't account for the amount of content, whether or not it was user-generated or editable or had the potential to scale up. At the time, I wondered why drawing was even supposed to be helpful. This was an honest rookie mistake; however, it made me skip the drawing part of the process for a good five years, which showed in my design work.

It wasn't until slightly later in my career, when I was working at Electronic Ink, a well-respected UX consultancy in Philadelphia, with a more experienced team with seasoned leadership did I understand the value drawing could provide. After watching my colleagues and observing their process, I wised up and realized that content comes first and everything else follows.

Once I started analyzing the text, its main points, and the underlying story it supported, I began to think about properly developing my ideas through drawings. I started thinking about how to better integrate the content with a visual experience in a proper flow and tone. I started thinking about how to incorporate large and small chunks of content into different sections of the website layout, thus creating a much better web page design.

Information Sources

This story from my early career focuses on websites; content is still king when it comes to a digital product's interface. When thinking about the components and screen-based elements in your UX drawing, think about the information that will be populated in these elements.

If you're not working with static content, then a lot of questions will arise. Where will it come from? Is it available today? How often will it be updated? Is it necessary to show when it was last updated? What is the plan for maintaining the content moving forward?

If content is going to be user-generated, then there are different scenarios we will have to account for. When sharing our drawings with our colleagues, we must speak to these scenarios. Let's imagine we're creating an e-commerce site for selling digital cameras and we're planning on featuring a customer reviews widget at the bottom of each product page, as drawn in the example in Figure 9.5.

Since customer reviews are user-generated, it's likely that some products may have a lot of reviews. Some may not have any at all. What does that empty state look like when there aren't any reviews? We should consider these situations, as depicted in Figure 9.6.

These are just some examples of the questions and scenarios that may be raised by your colleagues, especially when it comes to content and its source. Early on in the process, you don't have to flesh out all the fine details, but it is important to start considering them, as these considerations will help your teammates get on board with your ideas much more quickly. Let's look at a few more ways to ground your ideas in reality.

FIGURE 9.5

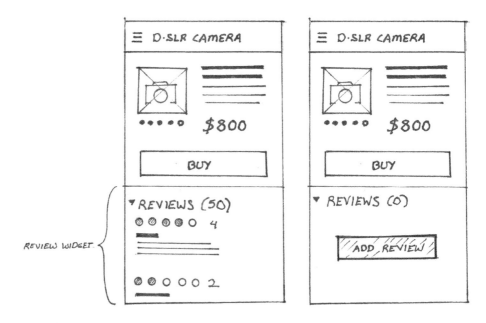

FIGURE 9.6

Interface Patterns and Widgets

Let's continue to expand on this content-centric approach to design. It's necessary to consider the volume of content and text you may be displaying in your digital product, app, or website. Let's revisit the previous product reviews widget example. In this case, since content will be user-generated, and the lengths of the reviews will vary greatly, it will be important to consider scale.

Each review can be lengthy, especially ones posted by people who are dissatisfied with the product. It's important to account for this in the drawing and consider how long reviews might be handled. A simple scroll bar may work, or applying a Show More label or an expand control within each review may be helpful (Figure 9.7). Even if you don't want to decide on a solution in the drawing, it's worth annotating. It's essential to show that you've considered these scenarios when sharing with your colleagues.

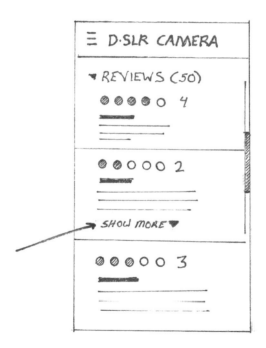

FIGURE 9.7

Also consider the volume of reviews. In this case, I'd anticipate a lot. Will the reviews fall on multiple pages, or will they load progressively? Alluding to how the widget handles high volumes of information, as depicted in Figure 9.8, will be helpful.

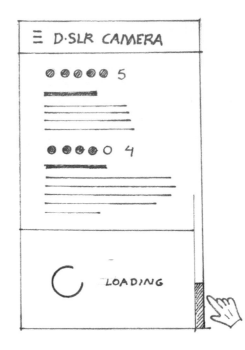

FIGURE 9.8

Reviewing Data

Considering scale is especially important when designing dashboards and visualizations. Let's imagine we're going to use a visualization to provide a key insight or answer an important question a user is asking of the data. First, understanding the size of the data set is important. Reviewing real data sets up front will influence the decision making here. Will there be an order of one, tens, hundreds, thousands, or millions of data points in the visualization?

Let's imagine we're creating a visualization that shows event occurrences over time. If we're dealing with a limited set of events, let's say on the order of tens of events, and the duration of each event is important to the user, we might represent blocks drawn on a swimlane. Each block represents an event occurrence and its length represents its duration, as you will see in Figure 9.9. We can even get an impression of cases when events overlap. This, of course, only will work when dealing with a very limited set of events.

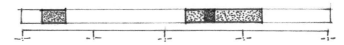

FIGURE 9.9

If we're going to show millions of event occurrences, and it's more important for someone to see unexpected spikes and dips in those occurrences, the aforementioned swimlane likely won't work. Showing thousands of events on a single swimlane would likely not be readable. Instead, histograms, like the one illustrated in Figure 9.10, are a more scalable solution and can be used to render an infinite amount of events. They also do a better job of highlighting unexpected trends, spikes, and dips in event occurrences.

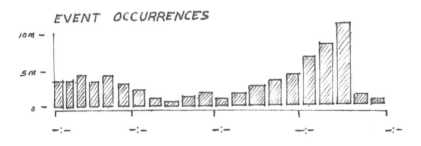

FIGURE 9.10

If we're going to show trends over time and we know there's a lot of data and we have limited space to show the graph, perhaps we should include an area chart (Figure 9.11) in our drawing instead of a histogram or bar chart. Line charts are more readable as sparklines than histograms.

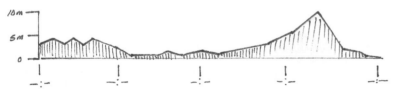

FIGURE 9.11

Knowing the data set and considering how it will scale up or down in your chart will enable you to make more realistic design decisions, even early on in your process when you're just sketching out your initial ideas. These considerations will make your drawing that much more realistic, and they'll make your ideas more concrete when it comes time to share with the rest of your team.

Show Something New—Start the Conversation

While you should always be ready to discuss how your hand-drawn proposal considers real-world constraints, it's sometimes nice to throw a few blue sky ideas into your presentations that demonstrate a breadth of thinking or provide a fresh perspective. You can sprinkle these big ideas into your presentation as you deem necessary. Who knows? Maybe it will lead to a meaningful change to your product's road map. The nice thing about a drawing is that it doesn't require a lot of investment. I typically use drawings as a conversation starter. If you decide to do this, just be ready to explain the constraint that needs to be removed in order to get to this state. For example, "if we had access to X we can now do Y as depicted in this concept sketch."

As you continue to include drawing in your process, you'll start to gain an understanding of the people you're working with and how much detail you'll need to provide. If your teammates are more visionary in nature, then you may not need to provide as many explanations. If they're people who aren't used to working with drawings, then it will be important to make the drawings as concrete as possible by clearly describing how the proposed drawing respects real-world constraints and scenarios. These people may rely on more detailed drawings and annotations to understand your big idea.

FIGURE 9.12

INVOKING EMOTION

There will be times, perhaps in a stakeholder meeting, when you're using drawings to sell your ideas. When doing this, it's important to pull out all the stops and consider some ways in which your audience will subconsciously connect with your drawings. Let's take a look at a few hacks that can accomplish this.

First and foremost, I always try to invoke a feeling of positivity in my teammates. I've always had an appreciation for wristwatches. Have you ever noticed that on watch websites and advertisements, the watch always reads 10:10, as drawn in Figure 9.12?

The visual shape of the hands projects a feeling of positivity. We can use similar tricks in our digital product drawings. If we look back at some of the elements in our visual language, we can draw them in a very specific way to do this. Let's look at the charts in Figure 9.13. Notice how the bars and lines increase in height toward the right of the chart.

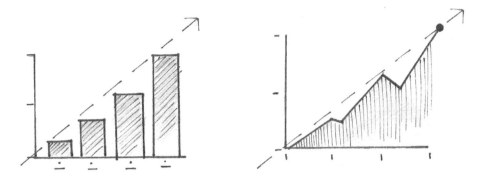

FIGURE 9.13

This can invoke a feeling of positivity through implicit forward progress and upward movement. We can apply these same techniques to texture and shading. For example, let's look at the inbox drawing in Figure 9.14. Notice how the shading used in the circular profile avatar images moves in an upward direction from left to right? This tiny detail is easily overlooked but contributes to that positive vibe the viewer may experience when looking at it.

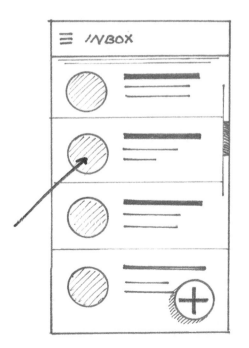

FIGURE 9.14

Finally, let's look at the same inbox example, but this time, let's focus on the elevated floating action button as highlighted by the arrow in Figure 9.15.

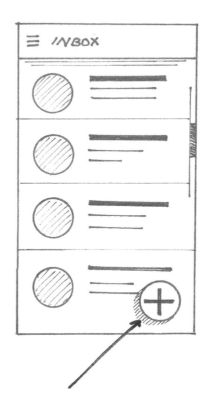

FIGURE 9.15

Notice the direction of the hatching lines I used to show elevation? They're also moving an upward direction, again invoking that same positive feeling.

Next, as humans, our need for balance is the most important psychological and psychical influence on us. In her book *A Primer in Visual Literacy*, Donis A. Dondis (1973, 22) describes the importance of balance in great detail. Equilibrium becomes our firmest and strongest visual reference, both our conscious and unconscious bias for making visual judgements. Items that appear to be unstable create visual stress. As humans, we subconsciously evaluate the stability of forms by imposing a vertical and horizontal axis on the forms we see, as depicted in Figure 9.16. The slightest angle of rotation will even throw off this sense of imposed balance, causing this stress. Notice how the drawing on the right, which isn't level, gives off a more stressful vibe than the left image, which is level in nature?

Unless implying animation, or drawing a very important screen element, it's important to ensure that all items in our product drawings appear structurally sound, as depicted in Figure 9.17. In this scenario, the image on the left appears structurally sound. The circular profile images in the list view are aligned and stacked on top of each other. Compare that to the image on the right, which appears unstable. The lack of alignment in the circular profile images makes the list appear top heavy. This will also cause visual stress. Caring for alignments and small structural details like this will enable you to instill a sense of relaxation in your teammates when they're looking at your drawing.

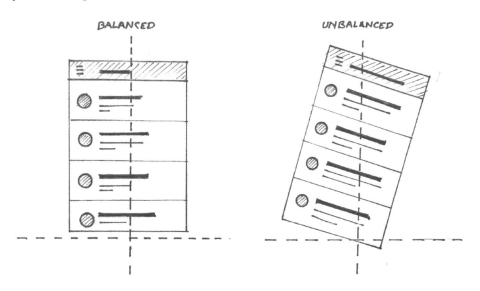

FIGURE 9.16

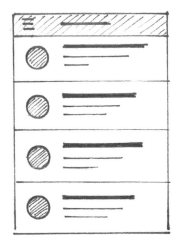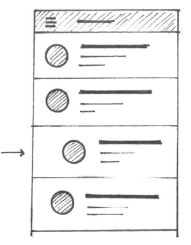

FIGURE 9.17

All of these techniques are very subtle, yet they can play a powerful role in establishing a positive first impression in a viewer. First impressions are important. They are formed within milliseconds of first seeing a drawing. They can last for months (Gunaydin, Selcuk, and Zayas 2017) and affect personal judgments even in the presence of contradictory evidence about the individual (Rydell and McConnell 2006). This is why it's important to consider these fine, seemingly trivial details when creating a digital product drawing to share with colleagues, especially influential stakeholders.

ADAPTING THE VISUAL LANGUAGE

Speaking of knowing your audience, there are some cases where you may have to adapt your visual language to something that's familiar to them. Let's go back to an exercise we reviewed in Chapter 2, "Reframing Our Thinking," where we explored ways to represent the values of 7 and 14. In one of the examples, we represented the values of 7 and 14 using a clock display as depicted in Figure 9.18.

FIGURE 9.18

When you first saw the clock drawings, was it obvious that they represented the values of 7 and 14? It's likely that this drawing won't make sense for most people living in America that are not in the military or working in healthcare. This drawing will read as 2 instead of 14. There are better, more reliable ways to represent the values of 7 and 14 to these people, as depicted in Figure 9.19.

FIGURE 9.19

Let's review an actual example of a time when I had to adapt the visual language of my drawing. In 2012, I spent a lot of time working with a popular investment banking firm in New York City. As a result of the Dodd-Frank Act and the great recession of 2008, the US Securities Exchange Commission (SEC) mandated changes in how banks develop and launch new financial products. The current process was tedious, and bloated, and no one knew exactly how to complete it.

This was an intense project to say the least. The stakeholder team spent several weeks trying to describe the problem to us. It was so complex, we kept getting hung up on various points in their process. The team was currently using traditional workflow diagrams to communicate the steps in their product review process. Figure 9.20 shows a very high-level example of a workflow diagram.

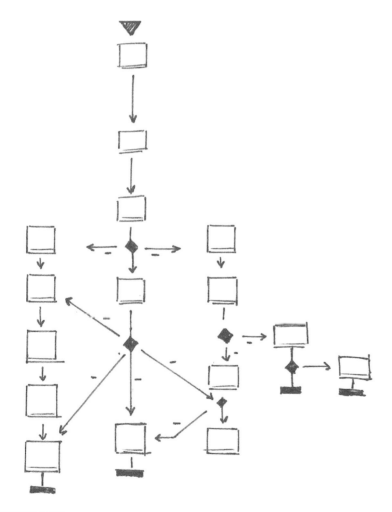

FIGURE 9.20

These diagrams were so complex, and no one in the stakeholder group understood the underlying visual language. Opportunities for collaboration and gathering feedback were missed simply because people couldn't understand it.

I quickly realized that we needed a new way to express the same idea. At one point, I started to think about how visual language might be applied in a way that can get everyone on the same page. After several design workshops, we mapped out a new, ideal process.

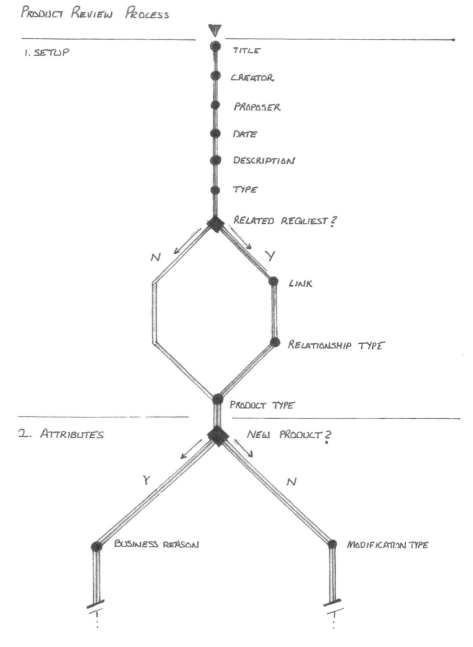

FIGURE 9.21

To communicate the new workflow, I tried taking cues from the visual language of subway maps. After all, most of the stakeholders lived in London, New York, or Tokyo, all cities with prominent subway systems. By using this familiar visual metaphor, the team would better understand our proposal for the redesign of this complex process.

By adopting a station stop and train line metaphor, we were able to illustrate how a new product approval process could be designed to adapt to each user. The resulting map depicts the data collected by a product proposer. Figure 9.21 depicts part of this subway map. The map represents possible tracks through a long proposal form. The map also highlights the most influential steps in the review process.

We used the metaphor to highlight special requirements necessary for each step. Since we were building a giant submission form based on this process, we could also start to illustrate ways in which the data would be entered and captured in the product. We took cues from how subway diagrams highlight special features like elevators, transfer walkways, and pay phones (back when that was a thing). Express tracks and local routes with more stops (Figure 9.22) illustrated areas where additional information would need to be captured based on previous input.

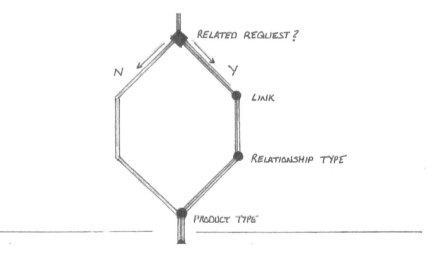

FIGURE 9.22

We used colors and shading (Figure 9.23) to represent different train lines and transfer points so the team could follow the main possible routes through the process.

Unlike with the traditional workflow diagram, using this familiar visual language to express both requirements and workflows meant diverse users could interpret our design even when we were not there to present it ourselves. Expressed in a familiar idiom that transcended text, it was much easier for our audience to offer feedback and ultimately buy in. Not only did this visual language augment the collaboration between research, design, content strategy, and development, it earned the appreciation of the client's IT team. As a result, the map became the IT department's requirements document of record.

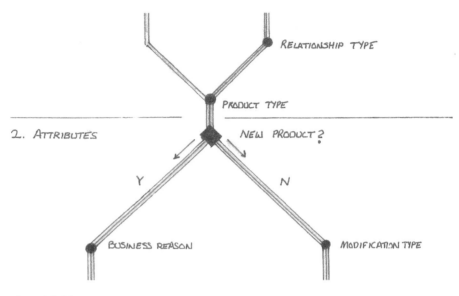

FIGURE 9.23

This is just one example of how changing the symbols, icons, and visual language used in a diagram drastically changed my team's perception of the same idea. There will be times when you'll have to consider this. As you become more comfortable with drawing, and as you continue to develop your visual library, you'll be able to come up with more ways to modify it based on your audience and their perspective.

WAYFINDING AND LANDMARKS

Since we're using drawing to develop and share new ideas with our colleagues, it's important to help them maintain a sense of orientation within the flow or storyboard. After all, this is the first time they're seeing your new idea. Just as in a well-designed mobile app or visualization, it's necessary to enable someone to understand where they came from, how they got here, and where they can go. In Chapter 8, "Using Flows to Tell Stories," we covered techniques used to do this. Showing mini maps and numerical labels next to screen-based drawings will start to give your colleagues a sense of location within your drawings. This is a good start.

Landmarks are another orientation mechanism, and they're used in several modern-day experiences. Disney Imagineers placed a large castle landmark (Figure 9.24) at the central hub of their parks. It's the tallest structure in the park, and visible from nearly everywhere.

FIGURE 9.24

Upon entering the park, guests experience a carefully engineered sight line to this castle, as depicted in Figure 9.25. From this perspective, the castle draws guests down the main corridor and into the other areas of the park. No matter where you are in the park, you can always enjoy a line of sight to the castle.

Once guests find their way to the other sections of the park, behind this landmark, they always have a sight line back to it, thus having a way to get back to the entrance corridor. This sight line, or view of the castle, is a crucial mechanism for wayfinding throughout the park. It gives guests a sense of location and orientation. Because of this, Disney was able to minimize the use of signage in these parks.

We can use these same wayfinding techniques in our digital product drawings. When creating drawings to share with your teammates, you should consider how you may use visual landmarks within your drawings to enable your colleagues to remain oriented within your ideas. This can reduce the need to add extraneous text to your drawings. Your result will have less clutter and make it easier to convey the essence of your idea.

FIGURE 9.25

Let's look at the example coming up in Figure 9.26. This flow depicts a single screen with a rich set of features. Notice how at the bottom of each drawing, we can see navigation tabs. The selected tab always remains in the same position throughout the experience. We can consider these tabs as a key landmark. They're going to remain stationary, and like the Disney castle, and no matter what screen drawing we're focusing on, we will always be able to see them and know where we are.

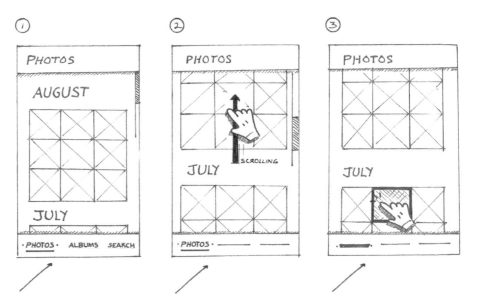

FIGURE 9.26

Once the tabs are established as a landmark, I'll start removing some of the details within that landmark in later screens. This is because focus typically shifts from the global navigation to details and features of the specific screen we're on. Doing this enables us to focus on the more important details of each specific screen drawing without adding unnecessary noise. In the example, you'll notice that I included all of the labels for the tab navigation up front. In the following screens I remove the labels for unselected tabs but make sure the selected tab is always in the same location. This removes noise from the drawing and brings focus to the interaction at hand.

Just as in Disney parks, as we move past the castle and deeper into the park, we start focusing on the details and attractions in our local area of the park. We don't need to see all the details of the castle. We just know it's there and that's good enough.

Another example of providing great wayfinding is to reuse key visual elements in our transition from one screen to another. Let's go back to our inbox example, shown in Figure 9.27.

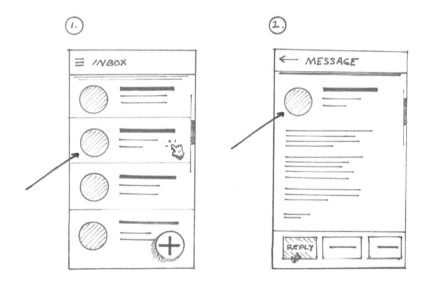

FIGURE 9.27

For this example, we're going to focus on the first two screens. Let's take a look at the objects highlighted by the arrows in Figure 9.27. Notice how the elements in the list item including the circular profile icon, list item title, and subtitle text on the left are reused in the image on the right. These same items appear in the same arrangement and form header on the message screen on the right. Notice how they're drawn the same way across drawings. For instance, the same shading technique was used for the avatar image. The title and subtitle lines are similar in length relative to each other. Considering details like this will help someone better understand your idea.

Now, taking a step back for a minute, let's not forget that reusing screen elements isn't only good for your drawing process, it has much greater benefits to the outcome we're striving for. Reusing screen elements across an interaction like this will ultimately improve usability of the app you're developing.

CHOREOGRAPHY AND TIMING

In some cases, the order in which elements of the drawing are introduced can help our teammates better understand the problem space, our ideas, and the ultimate solution. New items can be introduced as we turn pages in a printed presentation. They can be introduced over the course of several slides in a digital presentation deck, or they can be drawn in a specific order on a whiteboard in front of a crowd. Let's go back to the anecdote shared by professor emeritus Dan Boyarski from Carnegie Mellon University. If you recall from Chapter 1, "Why Draw?" we recounted a time when Professor Boyarski invited students to describe a problem using the whiteboard. One student explained how her group was trying to find an effective way for these people to talk to each other as they control barge traffic on the rivers, as illustrated by the drawing in Figure 9.28.

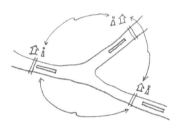

FIGURE 9.28

Boyarski describes the drawing being a useful element in describing the problem. He also went on to explain that what was even more valuable was the way the story and drawing unfolded together. This really enabled the rest of the class to understand the problem.

For example, the presenter started off by establishing that her group was evaluating barges traveling up and down the three rivers by drawing these elements first. This worked like an establishing shot in a movie or an orienter panel in a comic. It helped the class all agree on the setting and context. It helped the students gain a shared understanding of the problem space. They could see that they were discussing the efficiency of ship traffic on three intersecting rivers, as illustrated in Figure 9.29.

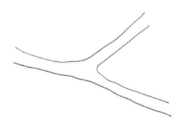

FIGURE 9.29

The student gradually introduced additional constraints and complexities into the problem by drawing the locks. Representing the locks as lines barricading the boats from proceeding (Figure 9.30), while telling the class that only one boat can pass through at a time brought up a critical bottleneck in the flow of ships up and down the three rivers. Showing the barges and locks initiated the tension of the underlying narrative.

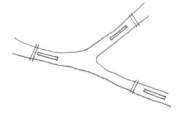

FIGURE 9.30

Finally, adding the control stations and people brought a human element to the story, as drawn in Figure 9.31. It was also drawn when the presenter got to the climax, or peak, of the story.

The final addition to the drawing outlined the opportunity that would solve the aforementioned pain point, which was enabling the people controlling the locks to better communicate and plan the flow of traffic, as depicted in Figure 9.32.

If we were to see the full drawing up front, we would've missed some of these key details that set up the story and clearly defined the opportunity to improve communication.

The sequence of elements added to the drawing can follow the arc of the underlying story you're telling through drawing. In his book *The Visual Language of Comics*, Dr. Cohn lays out several types of images that support this arc. In this sequence, the first elements of the drawing were our orienter (Figure 9.29). Next, we saw the barges locks drawn, which established the tension in our story (Figure 9.30). The peak, or climax, of the story occurred when people were added to the drawing (Figure 9.31) and we realized they cannot communicate with each other. Finally, when the final elements were added to the drawing, we see the story's release (Figure 9.32). In this final state, we see the aftermath of the story, or the opportunity to improve communications between the river traffic controllers, which was represented by the arrows.

When you're using drawings to tell a story about your product or service, think about how the elements of your drawing should be unveiled to support the different phases of the story arc. What should be used to establish context? What elements can be used to build tension in your story? What elements support the aftermath of the story? Thinking about this will enable you to unfold an image along with a proper narrative that will resonate with your teammates.

Because of the approach we take in this book, we can actually think about the timing and order in which we introduce elements into our drawing at the whiteboard. With some practice, you will no longer have to think about how to draw all the elements in your visual library. Instead, you'll be thinking more about how to compose them into a meaningful drawing. You'll even be able to draw them while talking to your colleagues at the same time. When you get to this level of comfort, you can begin to think about the overarching story and which items you want to introduce, just as the students did with the ship traffic scenario.

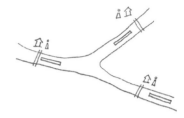

FIGURE 9.31

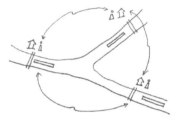

FIGURE 9.32

If the situation permits, and you want to share your great idea at the whiteboard, do a practice drawing on a notepad or sketchbook as your team is discussing possible solutions. That way, you can sort out which elements you want to draw and their importance and order to tell the best possible story. Once you take the whiteboard marker, you hold nearly all of the power in the meeting, so you'll want to make the best use of it.

PACKAGING YOUR DRAWINGS

My wife always says that it's all in the packaging. That's true for sketches, and considering where and how they live plays a major role in how people engage with them. I try to hang up my drawings, especially early ones, in my work space. That way I have a chance to live with them and subconsciously reflect on their content. As time passes and you become familiar with the work, you'll either gain additional insight into your ideas, or maybe contempt. Posting other material may aid the discovery of new explorations to consider (Buxton 2007, 154). This helps me develop better, more thoughtful ideas early on. If you have a dedicated UX space in your home or office, I'd suggest doing the same. If you hang your drawings in a public area, oftentimes you'll notice your colleagues coming by and looking at them, which usually leads to some fun impromptu conversations about the work. These casual interactions can lead to a great idea, and they can also help you become used to discussing your work in a casual setting. This can especially become useful when it's time to present your work to stakeholders in a more formal setting. I usually add sticky notes next to each drawing or group of drawings for displaying additional notes.

There are many ways to present your drawings. In some cases, the drawings can be dropped into a digital slide deck or multipage PDF. You can add additional notes in the actual slide, which can be nice if your handwriting isn't the prettiest. You can use some of the techniques mentioned in Chapter 8 for combining mini maps, process diagrams, and screens to tell the story of your idea.

If you're working on a formal design presentation, and you have access to a scanner, it's a good idea to use scanned drawings rather than photos taken with a phone camera. This will give your drawings a sense of visual polish and refinement. Doing this also ensures that there aren't any focus issues with your drawing and that all the proper details are clearly presented.

Just as we discussed in the previous section on timing and choreography, you can also introduce new elements on each slide to help people better understand the problem space and your solutions. You may consider recording your presentation in your favorite virtual meetings app so that you can provide a voice-over narration and change the slides accordingly. This works especially well if you're an effective public speaker and storyteller. It's especially valuable in those situations where you cannot be present to share your own work.

These are just some of the things you may consider when creating a UX drawing. This chapter focused on techniques that will enable you to create more engaging presentations that elicit the best possible feedback from your colleagues. Showing consideration for real-world scenarios and constraints within the drawings will help you build credibility among your colleagues, especially the engineers who will be building out the idea. Modifying your drawing's visual language and providing proper landmarks within each drawing will help your team better comprehend your idea. If you're selling an idea, think about how to subtly invoke a certain emotion from your teammates. Finally, modifying the visual language and considering the use of key landmarks and the timing in which you reveal elements in the drawing can help your colleagues better understand and even engage with your ideas.

CHAPTER TEN

MOVING FORWARD

While the technology, platforms, and services we create will change in the coming years, drawing will always play a role in developing new ideas. The systematic approach covered in this book will give you everything you need to continue drawing, sharing, and evolving your great ideas.

Throughout the course of time, you will have to make frequent updates to your visual library as people, processes, and technology continue to evolve and mature. Mostly any form or element you'll draw can be broken down into a few basic shapes. Think about which marks you can make on the paper to best represent these shapes. You can add techniques like shading to represent concepts like light, elevation, and texture to further describe these new elements in your visual library.

The underlying process will always be the same. From there, you can think about how to compose a story around your drawing and how to unveil it to your teammates. We covered several ways to create engaging stories through drawing.

The systematic approach to drawing can be applied to other areas and larger challenges beyond product design. Drawing can be used to help a patient understand an experimental cancer treatment. Teachers can use these techniques to help students better understand how major historical events unfolded. They can use it to help students comprehend difficult abstract problems presented in advanced mathematics and science courses.

Drawing can be used in the process of solving large-scale, complex problems like removing trash from the oceans, fighting climate change, and combating social inequality. While this might sound lofty, the possibilities really are endless here.

Reflecting on writing this book, I used over 500 sheets of paper and created over 300 drawings. Some of these drawings were practice drawings, and others were just bad ideas. If you're an environmentally conscious person, you may feel this is wasteful. With that in mind, let's not forget to recycle. If you have a yard, consider planting a tree. I did just that after writing this book, as depicted in Figure 10.1. I'd encourage you to do the same as you start creating more drawings.

FIGURE 10.1

There's something magical about a drawing. Sometimes drawings are the first time we're seeing form applied to a nascent idea. They can bring people together and start a meaningful conversation. They can inspire bigger ideas in a low-risk setting.

Now that I've hopefully made drawing more approachable for you, I hope you'll consider making it a lasting part of your process, and always remember that the drawing itself isn't what matters in the end; it's the outcome it leads to.

WORKS CITED

Aban, Serra. 2021. "How to use UX Modals the Right Way + 7 Examples."
    UserGuiding, December 24, 2021. https://userguiding.com/blog/
    ux-modal-windows.

Biondo, Joseph. 2021. Personal interview, November 4, 2021.

Borbay, Jason. 2022. Personal interview, March 14, 2022.

Boyarski, Dan. 2020. Personal interview, July 9, 2020.

Bullock, David. 2021. Personal interview, November 4, 2021.

Buxton, Bill. 2007. *Sketching User Experiences: Getting the Design Right and the
    Right Design*. San Francisco: Morgan Kaufmann Publishers.

Crothers, Ben. 2018. *Presto Sketching: the Magic of Simple Drawing for Brilliant
    Product Thinking and Design*. Sebastopol: O'Reilly.

Dondis, A. Donis. 1973. *A Primer of Visual Literacy*. Cambridge: The MIT Press.

Eilers, Søren. 2005. "A LEGO Counting Problem." Last modified April 2005.
    http://web.math.ku.dk/~eilers/lego.html.

Eisenhuth, Kent, Jeanne Adamson, and Justin Wear. 2013. "Making Complex
    Simple." In *Proceedings of the 31st ACM International Conference on Design
    of Communication*, 183–184. SIGDOC '13.

Gray, Dave. 2020. "Squiggle Birds." *Gamestorming*, August 3, 2020. https://
    gamestorming.com/squiggle-birds.

Gunaydin, G., E. Selcuk, and V. Zayas. 2017. "Impressions Based on a Portrait
    Predict, 1-Month Later, Impressions Following a Live Interaction." *Social
    Psychological and Personality Science* 8, 36–44.

Hassard, Steve, and Carolyn Knight. 2022. Personal interview, April 19, 2022.

Hench, John, and Peggy Van Pelt. 2003. *Designing Disney: Imagineering
    and the Art of the Show. A Walt Disney Imagineering Book*. New York:
    Disney Editions.

Hlavacs, George Michael. 2014. *The Exceptionally Simple Theory of Sketching:
    Why Do Professional Sketches Look Beautiful?* Amsterdam: BIS Publishers.

Leborg, Christian, and Diane Oatley. 2006. *Visual Grammar*. New York:
    Princeton Architectural Press.

Lima, Manuel. 2017. *The Book of Circles*. New York: Princeton
    Architectural Press.

Lima, Manuel. 2014. "The Great Wave off Kanagawa." November 24, 2014. https://medium.com/@mslima/the-great-wave-of-kanagawa-de2ea4b7871f.

Lupi, Giorgia, and Stefanie Posavec. 2018. *Observe, Collect, Draw!: a Visual Journal*. New York: Princeton Architectural Press.

Ortiz, Santiago. 2020. "45 Ways to Communicate Two Quantities." *Rock Content (blog)*. April 29, 2012. https://en.rockcontent.com/blog/45-ways-to-communicate-two-quantities.

Roam, Dan. 2013. *The Back of the Napkin: Solving Problems and Selling Ideas with Pictures*. London: Portfolio/Penguin.

Rydell, R. J., and A. R. McConnell. 2006. "Understanding Implicit and Explicit Attitude Change: A System of Reasoning Analysis." *Journal of Personality and Social Psychology*, 91, 995–1008.

Thorp, Jer. 2013. "The Human Experience of Data." *Interaction13*, January 18, 2013. Toronto: IxDA.

INDEX